CHRIST and the MONSTERS in Me

John Brian Passler

© Copyright 2018 John Brian Passler

All rights reserved. No part of this book may be reproduced, or transmitted in any form or by any means, electronic or mechanical, including photocopying and recording, or by any information storage and retrieval system, except in the case of brief quotations for use in articles, reviews, without written permission from the author.

The views expressed in this book are the author's and do not necessarily reflect those of the publisher.

7710-T Cherry Park Dr, Ste 224
Houston, TX 77095
http://WorldwidePublishingGroup.com
(713) 766-4271

ISBN: 978-1-68411-542-6

Acknowledgments

Thank you, Frances Watts of Southern California, and John Miller of Kansas for allowing God to use you as lights for His Kingdom when I was on my journey through darkness.

Thank you, Adela, my wife and ministry partner. God has used you to brighten my last eight years as my wife and irreplaceable partner in ministry.

Thank you, Marc Jankowski, for being my friend during my dark times of recovery and helping with the editing of this book.

Finally, thank you, God for your patience with me and for sending your Son to enable me to slay the monsters of my life.

Table of Contents

Acknowledgments iii

Preface vii

Introduction 1

Chapter One
In the Beginning 3

Chapter Two
A Year of Trauma 7

Chapter Three
A Different Child Surfaces 11

Chapter Four
Relationships 27

Chapter Five
Free at Last 35

Chapter Six
Off to The Air Force 41

Chapter Seven
Next Stop Viet Nam 49

Chapter Eight
Back in the USA 61

Chapter Nine
The Rush of Air Traffic Control 69

Chapter Ten
A New Awakening in Business 75

Chapter Eleven
California Here I Come 81

Chapter Twelve
Houston Bound 89

Chapter Thirteen
What's Life All About Anyway? 93

Chapter Fourteen
Saved and on a New Journey 101

Chapter Fifteen
Saved and Married but Never Quite on Course 107

Chapter Sixteen
Self-employed with No Partners 119

Chapter Seventeen
Off to Conquer Africa 123

Chapter Eighteen
Starting Over in Houston 133

Chapter Nineteen
My Calling to La Union? 147

Chapter Twenty
Moral Failure 153

Chapter Twenty-One
Almost at the Bottom 161

Chapter Twenty-Two
On The Mend 173

Chapter Twenty-Three
On The Road to Recovery 177

Chapter Twenty-Four
Back to Normal???? 185

Chapter Twenty-Five
New Year, New Country, New Chapter, New Life 193

Chapter Twenty-Six
Ministry Takes a Turn 197

Chapter Twenty-Seven
The Anchor Holds 209

Chapter Twenty-Eight
Life Levels Off 219

Chapter Twenty-Nine
What About the Monsters? 221

Chapter Thirty
The Process 233

Chapter Thirty-One
Counseling and Celebrate Recovery 241

Chapter Thirty-Two
Where Do We Go from Here? 245

"I've known John and witnessed the last ten years of his story. God has repeatedly intervened in his life in remarkable, unexplainable, miraculous ways.

This is a great story, with lessons that each of us can absorb for a life-changing encounter with God, and blessings beyond what we could have imagined for ourselves and those around us."

Marc Jankowski
Director of Celebrate Recovery
Houston's First Baptist

Preface

For a long time, friends have encouraged me to write a book because of all the interesting and exciting adventures that I have experienced in my life. Well, I finally have. But beyond the experiences on life's journey, the most amazing and fulfilling experience of them all is the substance of life that I've obtained through coming to know God through Jesus Christ. Because of that experience, I'm more excited to share the details of my journey.

The world has changed considerably in my lifetime. I've been blessed to live in a time when technology has grown at an explosive rate. I remember when television was only on for a few hours a day and only in black and white, many homes had party line telephones, (several houses sharing the same phone line) and the primary sources of news and information were the local newspaper and AM radio. I remember watching Alan Shepherd being launched into space for the first time for his fifteen-minute ride when I was in the seventh grade, then watching Neil Armstrong take his first step on the moon as it was broadcast on the screen of One Times Square Building in New York City. Then came calculators, computers, pagers, fax machines, cell phones and the internet. I'm afraid to go any further because there are now so many new forms of communication being developed so rapidly that I can't even name them anymore.

The world had changed considerably as well. I am one of those who remembers when *America really was truly great*, and we were taught so. My ninth-grade social studies teacher taught us that the United States was the world's largest creditor nation, now we're the largest debtor. He also taught us that if General Motors could have been ranked as a country, it would have been the fourth largest economy in the world. How things have changed. As amazed as I am about these changes, God has not been surprised by any of them. As we have supposedly evolved, our culture has pushed God further and further out of our world. And I continually wonder; how can we ignore such a vast, and incomprehensible God?

As I've journeyed through the highs and lows of life, there are several things that I've learned and a few I hope I've shared on these pages. My comprehension of God has changed a few times. When I was a child, my Aunt Hilda taught me about a loving God. Then, as most of us do, I began to seek fortune and fame, or I think, like most of us, I was really seeking peace of mind. As I grew older and "wiser" (so I thought), I questioned the existence of God. Then, when I came to the end of myself, or should I say found life's successes which proved to be dead ends, I finally came to realize that God was the only thing that really matters in the search for peace.

At age 30 I became a Christian and began a new quest to discover who God really is, which turned out to be thirty years of trying to make God fit into the box I thought He belonged in. I know Christian life in many forms: what it's like to feel that God is pleased with me; to be looked on by the Christian community as a role model, then after moral failure, to know the loneliness of rejection by those same people; and to carry the shame of having disgraced God.

At age 60, I began to know God as He really is and to understand what He expects from us. Since that time, I've been convinced of three things. God wants to have a relationship with us which includes speaking to us through His Holy Spirit. Our relationship with Him can only be established by spending time with Him every day. And finally, there is no situation, problem or circumstance that cannot be addressed and resolved through our relationship with God.

While most of this book is written to what I anticipate will be a Christian audience, I hope I've given sufficient explanation to spiritual events and happenings, so that even non-Christians will understand it and maybe be inspired to investigate Jesus for themselves.

Finally, some of my experiences you'll read about might cause embarrassment to some of those who have shared parts of the journey with me. So, to spare them embarrassment, I've chosen not to share some of their identities. There are also businesses and even a country that I have chosen not to identify for similar reasons. I apologize for the mystery and I hope those decisions do not detract from my story.

I have also made some strong statements and stated some strong opinions about events and actions of others. Once again, it is not my intention to embarrass, judge or get even with anyone. I do not in any way consider myself a victim and any statements I've made have only been made to tell my story and I apologize for any hurt that I may have caused anyone. *I strongly hold to the belief that God is sovereign and loves me, therefore, nothing can happen to me except by His hand, according to His plan and for His glory.*

Introduction

I consider myself extremely blessed that while most men spend their entire lives chasing worldly things that they think will make them happy, God allowed me to have and achieve all those things by age thirty. Realizing how hollow my search for those things had been, I began a new pursuit. The pursuit of God.

Now in my late sixties reflecting on the journey that that pursuit has inspired. I consider myself even more blessed. I feel God has filled my life with experiences enough to fill five average lifetimes and has finally brought me to a life that inspires me to thank Him every day for the privilege of being His partner in ministry.

It hasn't been a journey without struggles and casualties, there have been many, many of both. I deeply regret the hurt to others that my learning has caused, but I see that the struggles have only proved to prepare me for a life today of helping others.

As I stand on a pinnacle of peace, joy and a confidence of knowing that I'm doing what God had planned for me before I was born, (Psalm 139:16), I hope my summary of that journey will inspire others to make a similar pursuit.

God didn't save us just to go to heaven. He saved us so that He could make us like Jesus and use us on life's journey to change the world around us.

Chapter One
In the Beginning

I was born June 6, 1948, in Mineola, New York to John and Gladys. Growing up I was reminded each birthday that I was born on the fourth anniversary of D-Day, the allied troop invasion of Normandy, France. That day doesn't spark many emotions these days, but as a child, the price that most American families paid in loss of life during the storming of the Normandy Beaches in the name of freedom was still very fresh in everyone's mind.

Later in life, while reading, *The Chronology of the Bible*, by Frank R. Klassen, I learned that according to him, I was also born on the recognized anniversary of the Day of Pentecost. In more recent years, I realized that I was also born in the same year that Israel was re-established as a nation. For some reason, I feel blessed by God in learning that my birth was associated with those two events. It made me feel like God had a special blessing or calling in store for me.

I was the firstborn, and my first memories of my parents were that they seemed like such a happy couple. My father was a butcher, born in Brooklyn and from all accounts I've heard, was one of the best butchers in the New York metro area. He regularly made a point that we should always be the best at anything we do. He was a scratch golfer even though he only played a couple dozen times a year, an avid reader, constantly striving to broaden his vocabulary and an excellent craftsman. He made beautiful furniture, completed impressive and sometimes sizable home improvements, and he had a gift for gardening. He built a detached garage, an enclosed rear patio and added a full dormer on the west side of our house in Hempstead, New York. A dormer is when you raise the roof line of the attic to create space for additional rooms. After retiring to Florida, he worked or volunteered at a local golf course designing and maintaining the floral landscaping around their clubhouse. He was very talented.

Prior to marrying my father, my mother had been in the US Navy Waves during WW II. I think she was a nurse. For some reason, there was a death benefit put in trust for me and my sister by the Navy upon her death. I only knew her as a homemaker, wife, and mother. From what I remember she was the best at everything as well. She passed away when I was five years old, so there are not many memories, but during my time with her, I remember a woman that would be considered a superwoman these days.

I don't know whether she had any art training, but she was a gifted artist. I still have a painting of Jack and Jill that she painted for my room.

One Christmas, she painted a holiday picture in every window pane in our living room. There had to be more than one hundred panes of glass in the wood frame windows and everyone was painted with a different picture of a holiday scene.

Everyone raved about her cooking, although I don't recall food making a big impression on me in those days. I remember her loving my dad and loving me and my sister, Kathy, who was two years younger than me. She tried to make every day special for us.

I guess the thing I remember most, was that she was a good Christian woman. We were at church a lot with her, and she raised me by the biblical principle of using the rod. She had a little wooden dowel like a stick that she kept in the top kitchen drawer. It was about ½" in diameter and about fourteen or fifteen inches long. I was deathly afraid of it. I can remember distinctly as if it were yesterday, the arc I made around that drawer every time I passed through the kitchen. As I made my arc, I always kept a sharp eye on the drawer as if that stick would come out if I didn't keep a close watch. But even though my mother used it on me regularly, I never connected that rod to my mother. It was the rod that I hated, but never felt anything but love from my mother. The memories of that rod and my mother's love always come to mind when I see articles by the modern child psychologists preaching the evils of physical discipline for children.

As my story will tell, I didn't turn out to be a model adult, but while my mother was alive, she had me marching a fairly straight line while still convincing me of her unwavering love. I remember being told regularly by adult friends and family that I was a model child. One more thing about her Christian walk, this may sound strange to some of you, but somehow God impressed on me in later life that I was saved, (became a Christian), as a result of her prayers.

We were a very happy family. I have memories of things like going to the drive-in movie to see Abbot and Costello meet Jack and the Beanstalk, going on vacation to Kansas to see my mother's family and going to the beach. A few years ago, I went to a weekend seminar where one of the exercises was to try and remember the time when we felt the safest in our lives. For some reason, I remembered one of our trips to Jones Beach. My father was holding me above the waves just high enough for the waves to hit my dangling feet. I must have been three or four. We were having a great time until he accidentally dropped me. I don't know how long I was under the water, but I still remember having that experience of my brief life passing before me. He did find me in the waves, (if I was lost) and I remember feeling his hands around me pulling me up out of the water. For some reason, that came to mind as the safest moment that I'd ever experienced.

At age five, I started kindergarten at Marshall Elementary School in Hempstead, New York. I remember my teacher Ms. Eicorn and her sister came to dinner at our home one night. That was special for me. The only other memory I have of kindergarten at Marshall is one morning when Ms. Eicorn had to raise her voice to my class for being slow putting our toys away. She didn't even yell at me specifically, but the thought of her having to raise her voice was devastating for me. That may sound silly, but in hindsight, my reaction to that event was a total contradiction to the person I was soon to become.

Chapter Two
A Year of Trauma

Sometime in the early part of my kindergarten school year, my mother was diagnosed with cancer. It must have been pretty advanced, because she died before I finished kindergarten. That was a year that rocked my world, to say the least. Mother was put in the hospital and my sister Kathy and I were sent to live with our Aunt Hilda at my father's parent's house in Valley Stream, New York. It was an old house that looked kind of scary from the outside, but it wasn't too bad once you were inside.

Aunt Hilda, my father's older sister, was a widow and a single parent. Her deceased husband died while attempting to rescue two drowning men—the two men were saved, but her husband drowned. Aunt Hilda was a strong Christian woman who regularly talked about Jesus. I remember that she kept a picture of Jesus on her dressing table mirror. She was a saint in the eyes of everyone in our family and turned out to be the only real stability that I encountered while growing up.

Aunt Hilda's son Edward was about ten years older than me. He was extremely intelligent but growing up without his father was obviously affecting the direction of his life. It was the early 50s and rock and roll was just emerging. He was a teenager and had no real role models. He was not a bad kid, he was just looking for direction in an environment that offered no positive male influence. He was regularly my babysitter and took me along on his trips to the local malt shop where I experienced the teenage rock and roll culture of the fifties. I was a cute little five-year-old boy and a real novelty at the malt shop. All the teenage girls would make such a fuss over me. They would pick me up and dance with me to the jukebox music. That was quite an experience for a child my age, but I remember it as a good experience.

Both my grandparents were born in Germany so there was a strict German culture in the house. I remember it to be very intimidating. My grandfather was a stern, mean old man that everyone was afraid of. There were several things we were forbidden to talk about, especially my Aunt Margret, his oldest daughter. I never did really understand what the problem was between them except that she must have been rebellious and refused to knuckle under to his iron-fisted rule. Aunt Hilda would sneak us away regularly to visit Aunt Margret, but we were sworn to secrecy about even knowing who she was.

Then there was Georgie. He was really my uncle, my father's younger brother, but he had down-syndrome and was treated by all of us as a child. One of my worst memories was how my grandfather would treat Georgie like a dog. One time he threw him down the stairs. I think my grandfather resented that Georgie had been born retarded, and I don't think he ever accepted him as his son. So, I was now living at my grandparent's house on William Street with my grandparents, my sister Kathy, Aunt Hilda, Cousin Edward and Georgie. It was quite a crew and quite an unsettling environment. In hindsight, I might even call it traumatic.

I'm not sure how long we lived there. It seemed like a long time, but it couldn't have been because we moved back to our house in Hempstead before I finished kindergarten.

While we lived with my grandparents, I remember only seeing my father at night. He still lived at the house in Hempstead or I guess I should say he slept there. He would go to work in the morning, then go to see my mother in the hospital and then come and eat his dinner at my grandparent's house. It must have been late when he got there because I remember always watching him eat by himself long after the rest of us had eaten. I remember him looking very sad and tired as he ate.

One neat thing I remember was that Shaw Avenue School, the school that I was transferred to was only about one hundred yards away from my grandparents' house. I don't remember much else about the school. Just that it was close.

I made a few friends in the neighborhood. I remember Mr. and Mrs. Curry next door on one side of us and Mr. and Mrs. Bauer on the other side. They were nice to me and my sister. I can still picture their faces in my mind. I took good care of my sister Kathy. I don't know why, but I remember getting a lot of compliments from people about how I watched out for her and took care of her.

But, I mostly remember Aunt Hilda. Sometimes she would take us to the movies. She would regularly take us to church, or at least Sunday school. She was a Sunday school teacher. One thing that really stands out is our trips to the park. Usually, on the way back from the grocery store we would stop at the park and feed bread to the ducks and swans. One time we had to go back to the store because we used all the bread we bought feeding the ducks and swans. Aunt Hilda had so much patience.

During the time we were there we didn't see my mother much. She came from the hospital to my grandparent's house to visit us once or twice. One time a taxi showed up at the house and I went out to meet it and when I opened the taxi door, a saw my mother had fainted in the back seat. I think that was probably her last home visit. We made a few visits to the hospital.

In those days children weren't allowed to visit the rooms, so my mother would come to visit with us in the lobby. I remember us being in the lobby and her waving to us from a balcony window a floor or two above us. One time they let Kathy and I visit her room. I think it was because she was too weak to get out of bed. Maybe it was because they knew she was soon to die. I remember them letting us get into the bed with her. I remember that being a neat experience at the time. But I think that was the last time I saw her.

Believe it or not, no one in the family told me that my mother had died. I still remember one of my neighborhood friends telling me that my mother was dead. I remember running back home to ask Aunt Hilda if it was true. She said yes, but I don't remember ever receiving an explanation of why no one had told me. We were not permitted to go to the funeral. My father had my mother cremated. He put the can with her ashes on the top shelf of his closet in our house in Hempstead and life went on.

Apparently, my father made a deal with Aunt Hilda to take care of me and Kathy because she moved back to Hempstead with us and I finished kindergarten there. Not too long after moving back to Hempstead my father brought a date home for dinner. I don't think he told us she was a date, but she was. Her name was Ruth. She worked at the cleaners across the street from the butcher shop where my father worked. I think the purpose of the dinner was to get her approval of my sister and me. It wasn't long after that I experienced one of the most terrifying events of my young life.

My sister and I had gotten in the habit of storming my father's bed on Sunday mornings and getting under the covers with him while he read the Sunday papers. One Sunday we made our way to his room and found the door locked. We didn't know what to think. We ran to Aunt Hilda and learned that someone was in there with my father. I remember the struggle I had with that. I just couldn't get my mind around someone sleeping with my father and us being shut out. I don't remember whether Ruth moved in with us right away, but within a few days, after I finished kindergarten, Ruth and my father were married.

It had been a traumatic year. I started kindergarten in one school as a member of an extremely happy family. My mother developed cancer. I was transferred to a new home, school, and family that was far from happy. My mother died. I moved back to the original house and school with a new family unit. Then by the time I finished kindergarten, I had a new mother. What a year. Oh, I also now had a new older sister, Ruth's daughter Regina, we called her Genie.

At age six, life was starting all over again with a whole new family structure and more importantly, a new set of core values that would prove to be very difficult for me to adjust to.

Chapter Three
A Different Child Surfaces

At age six I seemed to become a totally different child. Like any normal child, I had always done my share of getting into mischief. As I said earlier, my mother used the rod on me regularly. But in less than a year, I went from a child that was referred to as a model child, to one that was referred to as a problem child. As time went on I was called incorrigible. I even remember one Thanksgiving in my teenage years being told that my grandmother thought I might even be retarded. That was devastating.

To this day I still wonder what caused the change in me. Was it the shock of my mother dying, the trauma of the changes in my home environments at age five, the dysfunctional family that we turned into after that or a combination of all those things. Whatever it was, I changed significantly. In a later chapter when I address the issue of *codependency*, I will speculate a little on what I think about how some of these events impacted me, but in this chapter, I'll just state the events of childhood and adolescence as I remember them.

For some reason, I don't remember a lot about the early years of Ruth being my new step-mother. I think she tried to be a good mother, but she was very much lacking in parenting skills. I'm sure that she eventually began to love me but really didn't know how to express that love. In hindsight, it was obvious that she had her own set of problems. From the stories I've heard about her childhood, she also came from a very dysfunctional family. She was raised in a small country farm community in Tennessee. I never knew her father, he had died years before, but I got to know her mother, Mama Etta, pretty well.

Growing up, I spent many of my summers on Ruth's sister's farm in Tennessee, so I spent a considerable amount of time around

Mama Etta. She was a very legalistic church-going woman who I always thought was extremely selfish and vain. I remember every time we had to travel anywhere in the car together, we would have to ride with the windows closed, (before cars had air conditioning), no matter how hot it was, so that her hair wouldn't get messed up. After being around her, it wasn't hard for even a young boy to understand why Ruth had issues.

As I said earlier, Genie, Ruth's daughter was also a new addition to our family. She was a good, responsible, well-behaved girl and a good student—all the things that I wasn't. She was also two and one-half years older than me. Many times, I wondered how much of a factor her diligence was in the changes in my personality. There were a multitude of adjustments for her coming from a life as an only child, but she appeared to adjust, and I remember loving her as a sister from the beginning. My father and Ruth had two more daughters, Debbie when I was seven-years-old, and Candy, when I was fourteen.

As life continued at age six with all the new changes, I almost immediately started having trouble in school. I was constantly being reminded that I was not living up to my potential and I was regularly punished for my behavior. I was once tied to my chair at school during lunch period because I refused to remain seated. I think that was in the first or second grade. The corrections with the rod by my mother were replaced by beatings from my father with a belt.

As I grew older, the belt was replaced by whatever was handy to beat me with. A few family friends speculated that I misbehaved to get the attention of my father. There probably was some truth in that. Ruth didn't spank or beat me right away. I really don't remember when she started hitting me, but I do remember that she would use anything handy as well. It started with a wooden spoon which wasn't too bad, but she broke so many of them on me she started using metal spoons or spatulas. I lied and stole so naturally, it was like I had no moral compass.

In hindsight, I think I was looking for my boundaries. I stole from anyone who had something I wanted. It didn't matter if they were strangers, friends or family, I lived totally for myself.

By the third grade, I started running away. The first time, I ran away to Hempstead Lake State Park. There is a reservoir there. I set up a little camp, but the police found me and had me home before it was dark.

In the fourth or fifth grade, I began shoplifting. I remember skipping school one day and going downtown and returning with two shopping bags full of model cars and, a full supply of model paints and brushes to paint the models.

One Christmas I received a stamp collector's album as a present. I made about a half a dozen shoplifting trips to the H. L. Greens, a local five & ten cent store and totally cleaned out the stamp collecting section.

When I was about twelve or thirteen, a friend named Gary asked me to help him with his paper route. While delivering newspapers, we also collected payments each week for the subscriptions. I began going back on my own to collect from people that I knew hadn't paid and kept the money for myself. Gary never said anything but stopped asking me to help him.

One of my most convicting memories is the time I decided to sell Christmas cards for *Sales Club of America*. I got all the sales samples and went out selling and collecting money with no intention of turning in the money or delivering the cards. I specifically remember one sweet and trusting old lady. I took her money just the same. I still don't understand how I could have been so cold and calculating at such a young age.

As I grew up, our community changed from being totally white in kindergarten to being about ninety percent black by eighth grade. The black kids were extremely tough on we white kids and I remember being terrified to walk home alone if I had to stay after school. My fear of the black kids turned into prejudice in my teenage years. I think that prejudice began from hearing my father's hateful statements about blacks. My father was extremely prejudiced. He always said that he would take people for the substance of who they were, and that was probably true, because he had several black friends, but he hated blacks in general.

In the seventh grade, at the age of twelve. I ran away to Washington, D. C. I don't remember why, but I remember seeing an advertisement in the newspaper offering tickets to the capital for less than eight dollars. I think it sounded like an opportunity for an adventure and that's exactly what it turned out to be. I snuck out of the house at about ten or eleven at night with my clothes in two shopping bags. I walked through one of the worst parts of Hempstead to the train station and caught a train to Grand Central Station in New York City. I arrived sometime in the middle of the night. From there I took a taxi to the Port Authority Bus Terminal and caught a Trailways Bus to Washington, D. C.

During the trip to D.C., we experienced one of the worst snow storms in recent history and by mid-morning all the roads were closed, stranding hundreds of Trailways travelers at the D.C. bus station. I think it was my intention to eventually continue on to my Aunt Pauline's farm in Tennessee, even though I didn't have the funds to do that, but for now, I was stranded in D.C. with the rest of the travelers.

By late afternoon it was announced that no buses would be departing until the next morning, so people began to make plans for spending the night in D.C. During the course of the day of sitting around the terminal, many of the people conversed and established bonds. I was sitting in a group of five young men including myself. They were probably all in their early twenties, one of them was a sailor, and he may have still been in his teens. When they made plans to share a room for the night, a room that turned out to be in a flophouse hotel, I was included. I remember sleeping in between two of the young men in the only bed in the room and one of the other men playing a radio all night.

Early the next morning, the roads opened, and everyone returned to their journeys, except for me, I hung out in D.C. I bought two gym bags so I didn't have to continue to carry my clothes around in shopping bags. I'd seen people pawning personal items in movies and on television to raise money, so I thought I would try to pawn my transistor radio. Sure enough, they gave me a few dollars for the radio. In hindsight, I can't understand why the pawnbroker allowed a twelve-year-old who looked like a ten-year-old to pawn anything.

But it added to the adventure. By afternoon for some reason, I felt it was time to move on.

My money was getting low, so I went to the ticket counter in the bus station and asked how far I could get in the direction of Nashville on the money I had. They told me Roanoke, Virginia, so I bought a ticket for Roanoke. I don't think I really had a plan, and in hindsight, don't really understand why I thought that might have been a wise move to go to Roanoke, but that's what I did. My inquiries at the ticket counter raised some suspicions with the ticket salesman and it wasn't long before the station manager started asking me questions.

It wasn't much longer before he was on the phone with my parents. I don't remember talking to my parents that night, but I think they decided to teach me a lesson and asked the station manager to turn me into the police as a runaway. I was taken away to what they called a children's shelter, but I think it was really a reform school for boys. There I met some dangerous characters who were in there for terms of punishment. One boy stands out because he was in there for trying to burn down a bridge. I think he was even younger than I was. I wonder where he is today.

I don't remember being there very long, maybe a few days. It wasn't that bad if you stayed away from the real bad kids. I don't remember ever feeling like I was in danger. I think what was considered bad in those days, doesn't come close to what we consider bad today.

One afternoon they called my name and told me I was going home. They put me on a bus and sent me back to New York City. All I remember about what seemed to be a long car ride from the city to our house in Hempstead was that the only thing my father seemed to be upset about was that he had to pick me up on his bowling night. I don't remember getting a spanking or even being punished. I had just returned from what should have been one of the most traumatic experiences of my life, but I don't remember any conversations or questions about why I ran away, not that I had any answers. But for some reason, I expected more to happen than to hear that I'd ruined my father's bowling night.

It reminds me that several years earlier when I was in the Cub Scouts, and our awards banquet was held on his bowling night as well. I was the only kid there without a parent. I clearly remember that to be one of the most painful experiences of my childhood. I think by the time I reached seventh grade and thinking my father's bowling night was far more important to him than I was, I had begun to learn how to stuff my feelings. I say that because in later years, as I began to deal with my *codependency*, I learned that stuffing our feelings is one of the primary causes of *codependency*.

I haven't said a lot about my father. I don't remember much about how he was while my mother was alive, which I guess is understandable. He would be at work most of the time and I was home with my mother and sister. As I have said, for some reason there's no doubt in my mind that he loved my mother and we were a very happy family. But after her death, I don't remember much happiness. My father continued to work a lot, maybe even more than before.

The most vivid memories I have of him, have to do with money. He was a butcher and I don't think he made a lot of money, probably average for those days, but he budgeted what he made and we lived a reasonably comfortable life. We went on vacations almost every summer. We didn't have a lot of clothes, but I don't remember being without anything. We lived in an average house, but he was always building and improving to the point where our house was considerably nicer than the houses on either side of us, though they all started out originally identical.

Financially, he was very security conscious, too security conscious for my liking. His father had gone into business and had lost everything around the time of the great depression. I think the memories of the financial struggles his family had because of the business failure caused such a scar on him that he had decided that He would never go through that experience again. There's nothing wrong with being security conscious, but it can be overdone.

What stands out to me was the contrast between my father and my millionaire Uncle Joe. Joe was the husband of my father's youngest sister Anna. He was a German immigrant with a very

German temperament. As I heard it, he and my father started working together at the Trunz meatpacking plant in Brooklyn, New York. My father continued with Trunz Meats and worked at several of their different retail butcher shops. He was a manager then, because of a dispute with the owner's grandson, was demoted to what they called an ice house butcher. My father hated the company and he hated his position, but for forty plus years, he stayed because they had a good pension plan.

Uncle Joe bought a butcher shop of his own from one of the competitors. Uncle Joe went on to become a millionaire while my father remained with Trunz until retirement. At one point, Uncle Joe offered to set my father up in his own shop and give him fifty percent ownership without having to put up a penny. My father turned him down for fear that if the business failed, he would have to ask for his old job back and would have lost at least a portion of his pension. That decision had as big an impact on me as my grandfather's failure had had on my father. I swore that I would never let an opportunity pass me by without reaching out and grabbing it.

Life wasn't all bad, I have good memories as well, especially the good times of our Christmases. Some of my best memories are about earning money and planning our gift buying lists with my sisters. Christmas was also the time for our annual trip into the city to see the Christmas show at Radio City Music Hall and have supper at the Brass Rail Restaurant. It was an all-day event. We would leave early in the morning so that we could get a good place in the ticket line. It was always bitterly cold, so we took turns standing in line. Some of us would stand in line while the rest of us would keep warm at the Horn & Hardart Cafeteria around the corner.

Through a child's eyes, Radio City Music Hall seemed humongous. In those days the Christmas show lasted four or five hours. There were several musical floorshows, the Rockettes did their thing, there was a reenactment of the birth of Jesus with live animals and finally, there was a premier movie. After the show, we went to the Brass Rail which seemed like an expensive restaurant and had dinner. It was always a great day.

On Christmas day, we would always visit my Aunt Anna, Uncle Joe, and my cousins Joey and Rosemarie in Yonkers, New York. Aunt Hilda, Cousin Edward, my grandmother, and Georgie would be there as well. It was always a time of abundant sweets and a great meal. Being a family of butchers, we always ate well. I remember one year, my father being so excited because we were having prime ribs of beef for dinner. That was his favorite meal, it turned out to be my favorite as well.

I really enjoyed spending time with Joey and Rosemarie. One Christmas vacation, I got to spend a whole week with them at their house. Aunt Anna and Uncle Joe were also my Godparents. Aunt Anna took that very seriously and always treated me special. She used to take Joey and Rosemarie on a lot of vacations, and one time when I was ten, she took me with them on an Easter vacation to Washington, D.C. It was several years before I ran away, and I don't remember that trip having anything to do with me running away there. We took the train to get there and visited all the sights. We visited the White House, Mount Vernon, the Capital Building, the Washington Monument and the US Mint just to name a few. We were there for several days.

Aunt Anna always seemed to be so patient with us. I can still see in my mind how her face used to change from a look of frustration to a smile of love and approval when we would ask for something that went beyond her plans. As an adult, I still regularly think about that vacation and how it supplied some of my favorite childhood memories.

I feel very fortunate to have grown up in a place where it snowed. I have so many good memories of playing in the snow, sledding, building snow-forts and snowball fights. Snow also offered the opportunity to make money. When it snowed more than about six inches, we usually got the day off from school. We'd spend the first few hours of the morning shoveling walks to earn money, then we'd spend the rest of the day playing. We had so much fun, I don't remember ever getting cold. I can only remember one bad experience. There was a bad snow storm the night before JFK was inaugurated as president. I got the job of shoveling a sloped driveway on that day. The snow was deep, wet and heavy. The job was hard, and the progress was slow. Not too long after starting, I knew I'd taken on more work than I had expected and for less money than what it was worth. I wanted to run away and abandon the work.

There was a big picture window overlooking the driveway. I could see the woman who had hired me standing by the window watching the inauguration and watching me. About halfway through the job, I realized it would probably take me until dark to finish and there would be no time to play. I don't know why I didn't just tell her I wanted to quit. Maybe it was because I was afraid that she would demand that I stay and finish, but when I saw her leave the window for a minute, I took off. I'd spent three or four hours working and had nothing to show for it, but I felt like I'd been freed from a torture chamber.

As I said earlier, I spent my summers on Aunt Pauline and Uncle William Campbell's farm in Tennessee. Pauline was Ruth's older sister. They had four boys, all of them were older than me, and the three oldest had already moved out on their own. Carter, or "Tumpy" as we called him, was still living at home and in high school. He was about eight years older than me, but I took to him immediately. As it turns out, my time on the farm with the Campbell Family was one of the most positive influences of my adolescent years. Aunt Pauline and Uncle William or Dodie and Pap as they were known, were strong Christians, even though they rarely talked much about God. They just lived it. They went to church every Sunday and almost every night when there was a "church meeting" as they called it in the Church of Christ. Baptists would call it a week of revival.

The church was only a few hundred yards from their house, so we walked to church most of the time when the creek wasn't up. There was a creek that ran about halfway between the house and the main road. Most of the time the creek was only a few inches deep and it was easy to drive across. There were also enough rocks above the waterline to walk across safely. When the creek was up, the only way across was on the foot log that was laid across the creek about ten feet above the creek bed. It was a log about twelve-inches in diameter with short boards, two- or three-inches wide nailed to it also about twelve-inches apart. The boards were to step on so you didn't slip on the log when it was wet. They eventually built a concrete bridge across the creek, but that was after I had stopped my summer visits. That creek supplied a lot of good memories of my time on the farm. During the years of my visits, my cousins and I would fish in it, swim in it, take baths in it and spend a lot of time just exploring, building dams and playing with all its different inhabitants such as fish, crawfish, snakes, and turtles.

Another unique experience I had there was the joy of using an outhouse and finding out first hand that a Sears Catalog serves its best purpose when being read. In the outhouse, the older editions also served (poorly), as toilet paper. I never understood why the outhouse had two places to sit. It scared me to death to use it. I was always deathly afraid that a spider was going to crawl up from underneath and bite me while I was sitting there. I got to the point where I preferred to go in the bushes until I used the wrong kind of leaf for toilet paper and acquired a terrible case of poison ivy on my butt. That must be up there as one of my worst experiences as a child.

I loved my times in Tennessee. Dodie and Pap had raised four fine boys and were not lacking in parenting skills. They established clear, firm boundaries for me while I was there which I usually honored, but I still often felt like a fish out of water when interacting with the local kids. They were, for the most part, Christian kids and I felt very much like a New York street kid when I was around them. Tumpy and I were together most of the time. I worked with the men on the farm most days and because I was so small, I had the easier jobs. I couldn't pick up a bale of hay, so I got to drive the tractor that pulled the hay wagon. I helped with the milking of their five cows, but probably spent more time playing and keeping Tumpy company.

The dirtiest and hardest job I had was carrying and standing the tobacco sticks that they hung the tobacco on to dry. They were heavy when we were carrying them in a bundle to distribute and they were about four feet long. To drive them into the ground, I had to lift a four-pound hammer over my head and hit the stick. Fortunately, we only harvested tobacco for a few weeks each summer, but it always seemed like a lot longer. I learned what hard farm work was like, but they always seemed to mix fun in with the work. I learned a lot from my uncles and cousins. I learned how to hunt and fish there.

There wasn't a lot of hunting during the summer, but we did plenty of fishing.

I went to church whenever they did and although I didn't understand much about the preaching, I enjoyed the singing very much. I mostly enjoyed playing with the other kids after the service. I witnessed an emotional event when a woman accepted Christ during one of the church meetings, and I went along as they rushed her to another church that evening to be baptized, because their church didn't have a baptismal pool. I don't remember those experiences changing me much, but they were experiences I'll never forget, so they must have.

Later in life when I became a Christian I was more able to understand what I had witnessed as a kid. I believe God was laying a foundation for my future salvation during those summers.

I had a few encouragers while growing up as well. Miss Edwards, my fourth-grade teacher asked me once what I wanted to be when I grew up. I didn't know, but she began to point out some of my talents and made some suggestions. I don't even remember what she said, I only remember her talking to me about positive things. In later years two teachers complimented me on my problem-solving ability.

In the eighth grade Mr. Van Houten, my math teacher gave us a word problem that could only be solved through algebra. We hadn't learned algebra yet, but he told us that if anyone could give him the answer before the end of the day, he would give them an A for the semester. I figured it out and gave him the answer at lunchtime. He told me that I was the only one that had figured it out in the whole eighth grade. He told me that he hadn't even had anyone in the advanced math class that could solve the problem.

Then in the ninth grade Mr. Silver my science teacher gave us a problem about a series of conveyor belts moving at different speeds. Again, I was the only one who was able to solve it correctly. I'm sure those two experiences impacted me because of them being memories of standout achievements, but I think they also stand out because those teachers and Miss Edwards were the only ones to recognize anything positive about me. Several teachers told me I was smart, but they always attached a few my faults to their statements which seemed to always overshadow their compliments.

About the time I returned from my adventure in the D.C. reform school, I began to steal money from my father's pay envelope. Back in those days, people received their pay in cash. Every Saturday my father got a little brown envelope about two inches by three inches, and on the outside was what looked like a paycheck stub with an accounting of what had been earned and deducted. Inside the envelope were the rolled-up bills and loose change in the amount of his net pay. When my father came home, he would put the envelope in his desk drawer where it sat until he made his bank deposit. I found it easy to just go help myself to a twenty or more whenever I wanted it. This went on for several years.

To this day I can't understand how it took him several years to figure out that the money was missing. He had a very detailed budget sheet of what was supposed to be going to the bank each week. I guess he never compared the deposit slips that my stepmother received at the bank with his budget sheet. He finally figured out something was wrong when he had a check bounce. He went back and audited his deposits for the previous years and found that there were several hundred dollars missing. I was never told what the exact amount was. Several hundred dollars is a lot of money, but that was especially a lot of money in those days.

The year I turned fourteen was another pivotal time of my life. When I returned from the summer in Tennessee, I had a new baby sister and I learned that we were moving. While I was gone, my sister Candy had been born and my parents bought a new house in Baldwin. It was approximately one mile from our house in Hempstead but was in a different school district that was one hundred percent white and about eighty percent of that, Jewish. I don't remember what I thought about the move at the time, but it didn't take long for me to start looking forward to it. Before school started I was also offered a job at a grocery store in Freeport, New York. The job was to help with cleaning and stocking the store. It would be working Saturdays only, so my parents encouraged to take it.

When it was time for school to start, our new house still wasn't finished so I had to start the ninth grade, in Hempstead. When they told me that I was only going to Hempstead High for a few weeks and wouldn't be getting a report card there, I made no effort to learn or study. I started smoking right away to fit in with the new high school crowd. What was supposed to be a few weeks turned into two months and as a result, I received a report card in Hempstead, and it was terrible. I failed four out of five academic classes. And what's worse is that I didn't learn any of the fundamental knowledge in any of my classes. So, when I started classes in Baldwin, I was not prepared. It was a tougher academic program than Hempstead, but I wasn't even ready for an easier program. They changed nearly all my classes to a lower track curriculum, but that didn't help either. I was more interested in fitting in than I was about my grades.

I never really recovered academically. I had never been interested in being a great student, but I was settling in and getting comfortable being a poor student. I was pretty good at being a clown, that seemed the best way to be accepted. I ended up failing Freshman English and History and had to retake both in summer school. I passed them both and could graduate junior high and start senior high the next year, but it had been a disastrous year.

One good thing happened. My freshman English teacher, Mrs. Spirakis was an advisor to the drama club and director of the freshman play. The play that year was *Cheaper by the Dozen.* They needed someone to play the role of the youngest child Jackie, and she asked me if I would audition. I don't know why she picked me. Maybe it was because I was one of the smaller kids in school or maybe it was that my freckled face was right for the part. Whatever the reason, I'm happy she did. To that point, I had spent most of my efforts trying to fit in with those kids who I thought were the cool kids. The drama crowd was a whole different group. Most of them were in the advanced classes with a totally different set of goals and level of intellect. At first, I was intimidated, but to my amazement, they accepted me and at least for ninth grade, I became part of their crowd.

As I write this, I'm trying to remember what I was thinking in those days. I think the only thing I was interested in was fitting in and being accepted. I would do just about anything to be accepted. I would clown and do stupid things in response to dares, I would even take abuse from bullies if I thought they would accept me. I don't remember having any thoughts about academics, present or future. And, I remember being very lonely. I don't remember having any role models and very few close friends from school. I had friends from the neighborhood, but because of my job and rarely being permitted out on weeknights, there weren't many opportunities to make friends with classmates.

My step-mother was very critical of me and my friends, especially girlfriends. She had me convinced that I was stupid and funny looking. My father wouldn't spend the money for much-needed braces and my stepmother regularly reminded me how crooked my teeth were. She used to say I could eat carrots through a picket fence. In hindsight, I don't really think her criticisms were genuinely what she felt, I just don't think she knew how to give a compliment or have a sincere conversation. She was so afraid of someone rejecting her opinion that she had to always talk sarcastically. The reason I can say that is because I had some of the same fears of rejection for many years.

Starting senior high school was yet another new adventure. There were two junior highs that supplied students to the senior high, so there were a lot of new faces to get acquainted with and new people to try to impress. I did a little better academically in senior high, but not a lot. I discovered that if I took lower track classes, I could pass with very little work. By my senior year, I was in a history class that I only needed to show up once a week and still get an A.

English was a different story, I failed sophomore English two years in a row. I was in an experimental class where you work at your own pace. I theoretically finished three years of English each year with an A+ test average both years, but they failed me because I never did my homework. I never could understand the logic behind that.

During my senior year, my grocery store job increased my hours from just Saturdays to Saturdays, and after school during the week.

The school allowed me to go only half-day and gave me credit for work experience. Unfortunately, because I failed sophomore English twice, I was one English class short of having enough credits for graduation.

I did well at work and everyone seemed to like me. I was given a lot of freedom and, as was my pattern, eventually started to abuse it. In addition to the cleaning they hired me to do, I began stocking groceries, eventually ordering the groceries and did some cashiering as well. I would regularly help myself to a few dollars from the cash register and called it an error in making change.

The owner of the restaurant next door to the store approached me and asked me if I would be interested in stealing meat and groceries from the store and selling it to him at a much-reduced rate. I agreed and probably made an additional $25 or $30 a week selling him groceries. Back in those days, $25 was a lot of money. I don't think my weekly paycheck was much more than that. As I write this, I get a knot in my stomach wondering how I could have been so self-serving and cold-blooded at such a young age. Was I desperate to have money, was I trying to beat the system, or was it that I just didn't care about anyone or anything but myself? I have no idea what enabled me to be so selfish, I'm just trying to paint an honest picture of who I saw myself as being.

While my parents did little to encourage me during those adolescent years, they did even less to prepare me for life. I regularly did things to embarrass myself simply because I didn't know better. I was rarely coached on the etiquettes of attending school functions such as parties and dances. Being very self-conscious, to begin with, each social failure pushed me farther and farther into whatever it was I was becoming.

When I was a junior, a young lady named Diane, invited me to be her date for her sorority dance. As a junior, I still wasn't allowed to drive, because my parents didn't trust me. In hindsight, that was understandable. Because I couldn't drive, we had to ride to the dance with her parents, who were the dance chaperones. That was embarrassing enough, but no one told me that I was supposed to bring her a corsage. She was the only girl at the dance without one. I can't remember ever feeling more stupid.

As my eighteenth birthday grew closer and closer, all I began to think about was getting out of the house and being on my own. I got where I hated my parents and just wanted to be free. They wanted me to work, but they never let me spend the money, they wanted me to save it. Saving money was one of the last things on my priority list, I think that's the reason I was so open to stealing. All I thought about was freedom and how much better I would be making my own decisions.

What's most unfortunate is that because they had been so controlling, they had not really done much at all to prepare me to be on my own. The only good thing that I feel I learned from my father was that if you are the best at what you do, you will always be able to find work. That has been a valuable ethic that has gone a long way in keeping me afloat in life. I have been successful at almost everything I've done, but I had to learn by making mistakes what to do with the success. As you'll see, rather than building on my successes, I almost always abused them.

Chapter Four
Relationships

To this point, I've focused mostly on the journey and not said much about my relationships outside the family. I had a few friends growing up, but for some reason, I don't feel like they were the same as the relationships that other people had.

I don't remember having any friendships before my mother died, but I don't think there's anything wrong with that. It's probably normal not to stray too far from Mom's sight at that age. But, for most of my years growing up I felt like I was restricted from having friends outside the neighborhoods where we lived. While most of my classmates were visiting with each other after school, I wasn't allowed to do that.

On a few occasions when classmates showed up at the house uninvited, my stepmother did not welcome them. I don't clearly remember the details, but it seemed like I was embarrassed by her lack of hospitality towards them. In the neighborhood, several of the families of my friends were very close. They met together during the holidays and exchanged Christmas gifts, but our family never participated in those gatherings or relationships. I remember my father and I going to a Brooklyn Dodgers game with my friend Neil and his father once. Neil's father was my father's best friend in the neighborhood, he even joined my father's bowling league. But I always felt like our family kept all the other families at arm's length, it was like my parents were afraid to get close for some reason.

Neil was probably my first good friend and we were almost inseparable during play time. He went to Catholic school while I went to the public school, but afternoons and weekends we were always together. His parents, Aunt Tessie and Uncle John as we called them, were like my second parents. Neil and his family lived two houses down from us. There was also Richie, Lollie, and

Bobbie, who lived in a house across the street from Neil and Susie who lived next door to them. We were all in the same age range and played together most of the time, but Neil and I were inseparable until eighth grade. Neil was a year older than me when he started ninth grade, he started going to public school and making friends with kids in his class further down our street. That kind of hurt, because we'd been so close. But we moved to Baldwin the next year, so it wasn't an issue anymore. I still think about Neil from time to time and wonder what became of him.

During elementary school the love of my life was a classmate named Linda, I remember having a rival for Linda's attention, a classmate named Gregory. During first and second grade we would both try to be the first to Linda's house after lunch-break to walk her back to school. We would both stop and buy her some penny candy and steal a flower from someone's yard along the way. Every day we would try to outdo each other with flowers and candy. I remember once one of us found a chocolate heart for her. I can't even remember which one of us it was. It wasn't even wrapped or in a bag, so it just got handed to her. In hindsight, I wonder if she ate it after being hand carried to her house. All I know was that chocolate heart seemed to both Gregory and me to be the ultimate candy gift of our competition.

From the age of eight until my early teens I spent my summers on my aunt and uncle's farm in Tennessee. My cousin Tumpy was the closest thing to a role model for me. As I said, he was about eight years older than me. He was very responsible and well-respected by everyone. I learned a lot about the farm from him. He taught me how to fire his 22-caliber rifle and taught me how to fish. We played softball together and had walnut fights, throwing green walnuts at each other.

I had three other cousins that I spent time within Tennessee. Jamie and Robert who were my step-mother's brother's boys. Jamie was a few years older and Robert a few years younger than me. There was also Cousin Dennis. He was my step-mother's cousin's son, and he had a bunch of brothers and one sister named Cherry. I didn't spend much time with his brothers, but Cherry and I spent some time together when she came to visit. I think she was a year younger than me, but obviously more experienced. She used to tell me a lot about how women, (girls), felt about things. She used to tell me about her romantic encounters with boys. She shared how she baited them to kiss her and how I could tell when girls were baiting me. Those were some heavy conversations for a very naive boy of thirteen or fourteen. Jamie was like Tumpy, very responsible. We did a lot of things together, but Dennis was the one that I remember getting into the most trouble with.

One of my most memorable experiences on the farm was when Dennis and I played rodeo with one of the calves in the barn. He was in an enclosed stall probably about ten feet by twenty feet. We tied a rope around his middle and rode him or should I say we tried to ride him in the stall. I remember that being a lot of fun. One afternoon after we were finished playing with the calf, we made the mistake of going out in the cow pasture to play. When we were close enough to the calf's mother for her to catch her baby's scent on us, she charged us. Fortunately, we ran in different directions, so she could only chase one of us. I ran for the fence and when I got to it, I was shaking so badly, I couldn't even climb over it. Fortunately, I wasn't the one she was chasing. Dennis had sought shelter in a big pile of brush and was shaking an old dead tree limb at the mama cow to keep her at a distance. I watched for a while then I finally thought to go back to the house and get an adult to come rescue Dennis. That was the last time we rode her calf.

Tumpy's older brother CW and his wife Jean lived in a town about thirty minutes from the farm and sometimes I would go and stay with them. I knew them well because they had come to live with us in New York while CW was an apprentice butcher. Jean had two cousin's that lived across the street from them, Buddy and Barbara. Buddy was my age and Barbara was a little older. Buddy and I became pretty good friends.

Once Jean took us to a community pool. I discovered just as I got in the pool that I had a hole in my bathing suit and was afraid to get out of the pool for fear that someone would notice. I must have stayed in the pool about five hours. Being from New York, I didn't have much of a base tan, and I got burned so bad that I couldn't wear a shirt for a week. I still have scars on my shoulders from that burn. Shy, stupid and self-conscious that was me.

Back in New York, I remember a brief relationship with Janice, a fifth-grade classmate. That was the first time I exchanged pictures with a girl. It was a serious romance. That's the first clear memory of my stepmother making fun of a friend. She always had to let me know that she thought Janice looked like a poodle dog. I hated that.

During the seventh and eighth grades, Carol stole my heart. But she was far more mature in her thinking than I. By the eighth grade, she started to talk about having babies and I still hadn't worked up the nerve to kiss her. I remember being at a party at her house in eighth grade and we were playing kissing games. Although I was sure she was willing, I was always too shy or scared to do any kissing. We remained on the brink of romance until I moved to Baldwin, but I was always too unsure of myself to officially ask her to be my girlfriend.

When we moved to Baldwin and I was in the ninth grade I quickly made some new neighborhood friends. John and Jimmie were my closest friends, they both went to Catholic school and were a year or two younger than me. Charlie and Billy were even younger, but they were old enough to play sports with us. We played a lot of softball and football after school and in the winter, we played in the snow. The Southern State Parkway ran right behind our houses, and there was a parkway overpass right around the corner. It was great for sledding. There was a big vacant lot a few blocks away that had lots of trees and a little stream that ran through it. We would make a sled path down the hill and through the trees and built a snow mound at the bottom of the path next to the stream. We would race down the path on our sleds and the mound would launch us over the stream. It was great fun. I feel sorry for kids that don't grow up around snow.

Jimmie and John and I used to go to the Mets games together too. We were big fans, and we went to a lot of games. After the games, we would wait for the players to come out of the dressing room and get their autographs.

After we had moved to Baldwin I finally had a girlfriend that I kissed. Her name was Barbara. I would walk her home from school just about every day and we'd kiss. I don't think we ever went out anywhere, I don't even think we talked when we were together. We talked a lot on the phone, but I think she was as shy as I was, so there wasn't much conversation when we were together. I think I was so excited about finally kissing someone, it never dawned on me that she might want to go out on a date. One time I called, and her sister answered the phone and she asked me if I was calling to ask Barbara out or just to talk. I think I was so embarrassed that I stopped calling.

I did a lot of stupid things in those days. I'm sure we all do, but for some reason, I felt I was always doing or saying the wrong thing. When I was in the freshman play later that year, there was a cast party and I had the experience of kissing another girl. Her name was Sue. On Monday at school, everyone was talking about Sue being my girlfriend. I don't remember what I said exactly, but I made it clear that she wasn't my girlfriend. I didn't know you were supposed to like someone before you kissed them. I think I was just excited that another girl wanted to kiss me. I think I embarrassed Sue. But being far more mature than I was, she rose above it all and was very nice to me. All through high school, I remember every time I'd see her, she would always greet me with a big smile and hello like she really meant it. Some people are classy that way.

I also made another friend in the freshman play. His name was Robert and he played Joe Scales in the play. We hit it off right away. He was in all the advanced classes, but we lived only a few blocks apart and started hanging out together. My parents didn't like him because he wore pink shorts sometimes and they thought he looked a little feminine. As a result, they forbade me from associating with him. They were very judgmental of all my friends. Robert was far from feminine. I learned more about how to interact with girls from him than I had learned from anyone else to the point in my life. And I don't remember ever really opening up to any of my friends about life issues like I was able to do with Robert. We were close friends till the start of the tenth grade, then we went in different directions.

I didn't remember any significant relationships in tenth grade. There were two different places that kids hung out during lunch.

Chats, short for *Chat & Nibble*, and the *Woolworths* lunch counter. I maintained casual relationships with kids in both places, but spent most of my time at *Chats*. I think those kids were thought of as the more popular.

I had one friend, Maureen, who I sat by in study hall that year. She had a boyfriend, but I remember enjoying our conversations in study hall. I remember being in that study hall when they announced that President Kennedy had been shot. Another reason I remember Maureen well is because she was involved, or should I say her name was involved in one of my more forgettable dating experiences. The job I had in Freeport was almost right next door to a big movie theater. I became friends with the manager and he regularly gave me passes to the premiere movies.

One time I asked Maureen to meet me Saturday evening after work to see one of the premieres, but she never showed. I waited for her outside the theatre a long time, but no Maureen. I think it had been arranged beforehand that my father would pick us up after the movie and when he did, I was too embarrassed to tell him she didn't show up, so I made up a story, something along the lines that her parents had already picked her up. He obviously didn't believe my story and started asking me about the movie. I didn't know he had seen it and I made up my description of the movie. Now I was in even deeper. I don't think I ever told him that she didn't show up. I preferred taking the punishment than giving my parents the opportunity to ridicule me.

As it turns out, I don't even think Maureen had realized that I had invited her out. And if she had, I wasn't bright enough to realize that she would have had to take two buses to get there, and what parent would let their fifteen-year-old daughter take two buses on Saturday evening into a questionable area of town to meet a boy that they had never met. Neither Maureen nor I mentioned the failed date on Monday at school, which is what makes me think, she never even knew I'd asked her out. Duh, another learning experience.

I tried asking another girl out that year with equally embarrassing results. Nancy sat near me in English. I knew she liked me and I called her to invite her to another premier. For some reason,

I thought to have passes to a premiere was impressive. In later years I remember being told that some people considered it cheap to use passes for a date. Anyway, when I called Nancy, I never dreamed that she would ever say anything but yes. I was caught totally off guard when she said no. She didn't give any excuse, she just said, "NO." I was so stunned that I just sat there on the phone speechless. Finally, after what seemed like an eternity of silence, I finally said goodbye and hung up. I was devastated. In later years I met a friend of hers that told me that she said no because she liked me so much she was afraid to go out with me for fear she would do something to embarrass herself. That was great to hear after the fact, but it would have been nice to know at the time of the refusal. It probably wouldn't have hurt so much.

All through high school, I seem to remember falling in love repeatedly, but, without much response from those I admired. I can't really remember all their names, but I distinctly remember wondering if anyone that I liked was ever going to like me back.

Then it happened. In November of my senior year, I was at a party and met Jamie, my first real love. Unfortunately, I didn't even know how to be in love. She was several years younger than me, but considerably more mature. We were together for the most part of six months, through April or May of the next year. Don't ask me why, but I kept breaking up with her for no reason. I guess I just didn't understand relationships.

Finally, after the second or third time, she refused to take me back. Jamie held a special place in my heart for years. I guess first loves are like that. There was also Patty. I'd met her in a junior year study hall. At that time, she was the girlfriend of one of my fraternity club brothers, Mike. (Fraternities, sororities, and their activities are mostly associated with college, but where I grew up, we had them in high school.) When Mike and Patty broke up and she and I went out a few times. Patty was from a moderately wealthy family and was driving a Thunderbird by the time she was sixteen. I was always intimidated by that. The first time we went out, you guessed it, we went to a premiere that I had passes to and we took the bus. I was embarrassed, but she at least pretended not to mind. There was another twist to our relationship. Patty's best friend Diane was also

Jamie's cousin and next-door neighbor. I've always wondered what kind of conversations they may have had concerning me.

Although I felt Patty was encouraging me towards a steady relationship with her, I always felt she was out of my league and never pursued it. She was a classy girl and we remained friends and stayed in contact for a year or so after high school. Jamie wouldn't talk to me again until years later.

As I left high school to start the next phase of life, I was still extremely shy and had very little self-confidence when it came to women. What was worse was that I still didn't have a clue how to act, should the right interested woman come along. But ready or not, life was progressing, and it was getting close to time to move on.

Chapter Five
Free at Last

My eighteenth birthday finally arrived and what an adventure that day turned out to be. I had a beach party celebration planned for Sunday, the day of my birthday and had purchased four or five cases of beer to share with my friends.

On the Friday afternoon before the party, I put all the beer in our spare refrigerator in the garage so that it would be good and cold for Sunday. At least that was the plan. But a problem arose on Friday night that proved to be a serious complication for my party plans. I had a regular Friday night curfew because I had to get up for work on Saturday mornings. I was on my way home Friday night on time to make my curfew when I saw two guys carrying a very drunk female friend of mine down the street. It was obvious that they were up to no good, so I went over to investigate. As soon as they saw me, they dropped her and ran. Her house was several blocks out of the way from my route home and I knew if I took her home I would probably be late. But I figured my parents would understand that I couldn't just leave her there. So, I took her home and that made me about fifteen-minutes late getting home.

Well, my parents didn't understand and they decided to ground me for Saturday night. I also had some fairly serious celebration plans for Saturday, the night before my birthday as well. I made several attempts to convince my parents that my reason for being late was for a noble cause, but they would not give in to the grounding. That Saturday night also happened to be a big night for my parents. It was the night of my father's annual bowling league extravaganza. My parents weren't partiers, but this was one of only a few nights each year that they would be out till three or four in the morning.

That night as they were getting ready for their party they warned me several times that if I went out that night, I would be facing serious consequences. But in my mind, they were being very unreasonable. I wrestled with what my response would be. I had not planned to move out of my parent's house when I was eighteen, only to start claiming more freedom. But, if I was going to follow through with my plans to go out that night in defiance of my grounding, I probably needed to be ready to move out totally. Even though the stakes were now very high, I not only decided to go out Saturday night, but to stay out for the whole night. I decided to stay with the family of my friends Babby and Bones, (those are obviously nicknames), for that night and for several more days until I could find a permanent place. I packed enough clothes for a few days and left for the night. I say for the night because I still had to come back in the morning for my cold beer.

About eight the next morning, Bones gave us a ride to my parent's house in his car to get the beer. I figured that if I got there early enough, my parents would be so sleepy that I could get my beer and be gone before they could wake up enough to stop me. Bones' car was about six or seven years old and had no mufflers. It had been painted gold with a brush and he called it "Golden Boy." It was so loud that you could hear it coming from several blocks away.

When we arrived at the house and opened the garage, we found that all my beer had been removed from the refrigerator and was scattered all over the garage floor. Well, to me, warm beer is better than no beer, so we quickly loaded it into the car. As we were about to drive away, my parents stormed out of the house. I could tell my father was mad, so I didn't wait to hear what he had to say. Between the time of Golden Boy's neighborhood entrance, the noise idling while we loaded the beer and our revved-up exit, we had woken up all the neighbors. They were all standing on their front porches nearly as upset as my parents about being woken up. By now, everyone in the neighborhood knew it was my birthday.

There wasn't much to remember about my birthday party, except that we had to settle for warm beer. We tried dragging it through the ocean water behind our boat and we tried burying it in the cool wet sand under a shady bridge. Neither seemed to work. Why we didn't just go buy some ice, I don't recall. Maybe they didn't sell ice in those days, or maybe we weren't bright enough to think of that. All I know is that we drank a lot of warm beer.

That was a long time ago and I don't remember a lot of the details of the next few days, but somehow my parents got word to me that I needed to come and get the rest of my things and make the move permanent. I don't think they thought I was bright enough to make it on my own and figured I would be back in a few days begging to come home. But that's not what happened. I did go back and get my things, including the new floor mats that I had just given my father for Father's Day. I gave them to Bones to put in Golden Boy. That was kind of mean, but I felt like I wanted to pay them back at least for the warm beer. I made my exit and I was free at last.

There were only a few weeks of school left, but I didn't go much. When Ms. Kloberg, the Dean of Students, heard that I had left home, she got in touch with me and told me she would have to suspend me from school for not attending but offered to let me take my final exams in her office. So, I did and passed all my classes. But because of my earlier problems, I was still an English credit short for graduation.

I've wondered whether Ms. Kloberg's act of allowing me to take my exams in her office was inspired by her desire to finally get rid of me or if she was truly trying to help me. As a student, I was probably one of her worst headaches. I think in those days my biggest problem was my attitude towards authority. In recent years, I've come to realize that I'm one of the few students from our school that left not seeing what a wonderful woman she was. I don't remember disliking her, or even disrespecting her, I just saw her as the authority I needed to outmaneuver. I guess back in those days, one of my biggest problems was that I had made up my mind that no one in life was going to be in my corner, especially those in authority over me.

With the school year ending, I had to decide whether to go to summer school to complete the missing English class or go on with life without a high school diploma. I decided that I wouldn't go to summer school and that I'd just take my chances without a diploma. I figured if I worked hard and became good at something as my father had always taught me, I would be able to take care of myself. Long-term career plans weren't even on my radar, only gaining freedom.

After making the decision about summer school, I really began to wrestle with what my next move would be. I had my job at the grocery store where I made enough to pay rent at the MacDonald's house, but not much more. I was going to have to do something to upgrade my income.

Shortly after I had moved out of my parent's house, I talked with an Air Force recruiter and took the AQE, (Airmen's Qualifying Exam), I didn't expect much from that. Because the day I took it, I had gotten drunk and didn't even read most of the questions. I just went down each page marking answers. I figured I'd failed the test miserably, and I figured that option was gone. But surprisingly, they contacted me. I must call it divine intervention, but they offered me a position in electronics training school.

I took the physical twice. Because the first time I failed the blood test because of my blood /alcohol level was too high from the night before, but the second time I passed. I was going into the Air Force to be sworn in on July 12, 1966.

It was the last week of June when I got the official notice of my induction and I called my parents to let them know that I was going to be fine on my own. They immediately invited me to move back home for the remaining days before my induction. But before I consented, I made them agree to some conditions. As I write this, I'm thinking, a normal person would have been happy to have proven their point that they could make it on their own, and to have received a concession in the form of an invitation to return home. But not me, I had to rub their noses in it.

I don't remember all the conditions that I insisted on except for one, that I wouldn't have to cut the grass. Now I don't know if my father was being cheap by not hiring someone to cut it or he was trying to make a point with me. But he had a serious allergy to grass pollen. He could not get near a freshly cut lawn without getting deathly ill. But when it was time to cut the grass after my return home, he cut it with me sitting on the front porch watching. I don't know whether he vomited, but he choked and gagged, with his eyes seriously watering through the whole process as I watched. Again, as I write this, I'm trying to remember what he may have done to me to make me hate him so much, but I thoroughly enjoyed his agony that day.

Chapter Six
Off to The Air Force

As planned, my parents took me to Fort Hamilton in Brooklyn, where I reported for induction on July 12th. As they saw me off, I think they were proud, but probably more relieved than anything. The inductees were sworn in and bussed to the airport that afternoon, arriving in San Antonio and Lackland Air Force Base later that night to begin basic training.

The freedom I thought I'd gained was over, and I was now in a place where it seemed like everyone was in authority over me. They put a fear in us and kept us so busy, I didn't have much time to think about freedom. We all shared an enthusiasm about being in the Air Force and began almost immediately bonding with others in the unit or flight as they called it. It was a tough time for most of us and you needed friendship to get you through it. My closest friends were two brothers, Vinny and Ronnie, also from Long Island. Although we didn't stay in touch after basic training, I remember more than a few times studying with them, while sitting on the floor in the shower after lights out to be sure we would pass our exams the next day.

I took the training classes and activities very seriously, but on the inside, in a lot of ways, I was still a rebellious child. On issues of personal discipline like obeying the no-smoking rules and other rules that I felt were stupid, I was still a problem. Somehow, I made it though. The six weeks went quickly with no serious problems and in mid-August, I was off to Biloxi, Mississippi for a year of electronics school.

I arrived at Keesler AFB with a new enthusiasm and the feeling of a fresh start. It was a very disciplined environment with a lot of inspections. Everything had to be neat and clean always. Cleaning was something I was very familiar with from my job at the grocery store, so I had a lot to contribute. I did okay in school, but I excelled in the barracks environment. It wasn't long before they made me a bay supervisor or "Green Rope" as they called it, supervisor over the living area for approximately twenty men. With the promotion came a little more freedom. It allowed me regular weekend passes without bed check.

I had two friends from my class at school, Ron and Sam, who had met some girls from the University of Southern Mississippi which was about seventy-five miles north of the base. One weekend they invited me along to meet one of their girlfriends' friends. Her name was Cindy and we seemed to hit it off right away. Dating a college girl was obviously a new and exciting experience and it wasn't long before I was going to USM every weekend with Ron and Sam. I really enjoyed those times. Everyone seemed to like me, and I was usually the center of attention. I was finally doing well on all fronts.

I continued to keep my priorities pretty much in order and while school was getting more and more difficult, I continued to excel as a supervisor in the barracks. It wasn't too much longer before I began to be considered as a floor supervisor or "Yellow Rope." That position meant the supervision of an entire floor of barracks dormitories, approximately 120 men.

Ron, Sam and I had started making money by driving men to the airport in New Orleans on Tuesday nights. Ron had a car and every Tuesday night there would be students from Keesler going on midterm school leave. Why Ron included Sam and me in the venture, I don't know, but we were excited to be included. It gave us money for weekends and it was a fun venture.

Because of the airport transport business, I was able to work some deals to get us covered for bed checks on Tuesday nights, so we started including a side trip to USM in Hattiesburg before returning to the base. Just to clarify what we were doing, let me itemize our travel itinerary. We would leave Biloxi at approximately 9:30 PM after classes and drive 90 miles to New Orleans, drop off our passengers then drive 120 miles to Hattiesburg for breakfast with the girls at USM, then drive 80 miles back to Biloxi. It was a lot of fun, but it was also taking its toll on my studies. By the time I was offered the position of Yellow Rope, I was starting to seriously struggle at school and even my barracks activities were beginning to suffer.

Fortunately, or unfortunately, I had guys covering for me, but they were starting to get fed up with me being absent so much. I remember my roommate Neil from Chicago really chewing me out one day. I accepted the position of Yellow Rope anyway, but I don't think it was even a week before my whole house of cards collapsed. I flunked out of school and was put in another barracks awaiting orders for reassignment. I had blown it again.

About a month before flunking out of school, I had stopped seeing Cindy and started seeing a young lady named Janet. She was also a USM student. Shortly after I flunked out, Ron and Sam went on midterm leave, leaving me alone, for a week with Ron's car. I didn't even have a driver's license at that time and being out of school, I had a lot of time on my hands. I spent most of my days at USM but had to be back by midnight for bed checks.

One night I was late getting back and was speeding down Highway 49 doing over one hundred miles per hour when the police stopped me. They hauled me off to a justice of the peace way out in the woods. I thought it was all over. When I told the judge, I didn't have my license with me and showed him an old learner's permit, he recognized that I was from Nassau County in New York and shared that he had been a judge in the Mineola courts for years. I then shared that my Uncle Dudley, my Aunt Margret's husband, had worked in the courthouse as well. It turns out that he knew my uncle and apparently, they were pretty good friends. He let me go with no fine and called it a favor to my Uncle Dudley. Thank God I had an Uncle Dudley.

When I got back to the base, I received a minor reprimand for being late and it was over. God had to be looking after me that night. That event could have been a major turning point in my life with nothing but negative results.

In late March I received orders for re-assignment to Duluth, Minnesota for on the job training as a security policeman. They gave me a week's leave, after which I had to report in Duluth Air Force Base, Duluth, Minnesota on April 15th, 1967.

Considering that I was arriving in the middle of April, I assumed that the cold weather was pretty much over. I was wrong. It snowed five more times after I got there before it finally started to warm up. When I arrived in Duluth, at the airport, which was also part of the air base, I was met by my sponsor and shown to my barracks. It was a depressing place. There was snow everywhere and a network of huge heating pipes ran above the sidewalks. All the cars parked along the street had what looked like battery charging cords connected to the buildings. I learned that they were heaters for the car engines.

Everyone was walking around in parkas and talking with what seemed to be very depressing attitudes and making very cynical jokes about the place like if summer falls on a weekend, we have a picnic. I knew they were jokes, but they weren't far from the truth. I remember there was still snow piled up between the runways in July. While I was processing into the base, I immediately put in a request for transfer to anywhere, but like it or not, this was going to be home at least for a little while.

I wasn't the only one there for O.J.T. There were about twenty others. After a day or two of processing in, we started classroom training on being a security policeman. A lot of the training was interesting. We learned about the protocol and ceremonial procedures of the Air Force, military law and both U.S. government and international security terms and perspectives. I still wasn't very enthusiastic about being a student, but they made it clear I had no good options beyond applying myself as a student. The class lasted about two or three weeks and after that, I was assigned to a security unit for duty.

I was also assigned a permanent room in the dormitory as well as two new roommates. One was Rusty, a musician, more specifically a drummer from Chicago. He and I crossed paths again several years later in Viet Nam. The other roommate was Steve and I don't recall much about him. We were assigned the largest room in the dormitory and had a good time fixing it up to make it more like home. Rusty had brought his drums along with him and started almost immediately jamming in our room with the other musicians in the dorm. Their practicing quickly became a problem for sleeping because we were on different shifts. Because we were on different shifts, we naturally made other friends with men that shared our same schedules.

After about a month, sleeping conflicts became such a problem, it was decided that everyone would be reassigned sleeping quarters to share rooms with others on the same shift. Believe it or not, during our time together, I got to be such a sound sleeper that I could sleep through the jam sessions in our room. Drums, electric guitars and basses couldn't keep me from sleeping. I think part of my sleeping ability can be attributed to me burning my candle at both ends. After getting settled and learning my way around, which didn't take long, I partied almost constantly. If I wasn't working, I was partying.

When I was at work I spent most of my time guarding fighter jets parked out on the flight line. That was extremely boring duty and gave me lots of time to think about my off time. I hated that duty because I was constantly looking at all the painted security lines in that area, many of which I had personally painted. One of the primary punishments for misbehavior in our unit was painting security lines on the flight line area. I spent a lot of time doing that because I was constantly in trouble.

Once I decided to grow a little goatee, something that was strictly forbidden. After about three days of growth, I was on my post when several of my superiors came by for an inspection. The inspecting officer noticed the start of my goatee and asked, "What are you growing there?" My unit commander said, "He's growing a paintbrush." So, I was soon painting more security lines.

I think the main reason I got into so much trouble was that my new job offered no mental challenge at all. There were some assignments that were a little more challenging. They were at the two missile storage areas, one was close to the base and the other was about thirty to forty-five minutes away. They were better duty because they were guarded by teams of men, so we had someone to talk to most of the time. We also got breaks. Half the men would be posted while the other half would play cards or board games. That work environment offered a lot of opportunities to make friends.

Then there were, Barker, Brown, and Giles. They were all in Law Enforcement, but on the same shift. Barker and Brown were also serious college students in their off time, but somehow we had time to get into trouble together. There was one time when we were arrested at UMD, the University of Minnesota, Duluth and the authorities called our wing commander in the middle of the night. That episode gained us a title, and as I later discovered, a bit of infamy. A year and a half after the four of us were gone and reassigned from the base, I needed to enter the base to use the Base Exchange. When he checked my ID at the entry gate, the officer asked me if I was the same Passler that was part of Barker, Brown, Giles, and Passler in years past. I almost choked. I knew we had caused our share of problems, but I had no idea how well known we had become. Of the three, I became closest friends with Pat Giles. He was from nearby Minneapolis and usually went home on weekends. I started going with him and over time our friendship grew. He is one of the few people in my life other than family that I keep in touch with.

Barker had a motorcycle and sometimes he would take me with him riding. One holiday weekend, I think it was the Fourth of July, we went to several public picnics and that night we visited a friend of his named Pauline. I don't remember much about our first meeting, but I remember we connected. I started calling her and spending time with her, and I fell in love with her as well as with her family.

Her mother, Mony, short for Monica, was a widow who had been left with eight children. She was an amazing woman and had an even more amazing family. There was so much love and fun in their house. I'd never been around a family like that. They lived on Park Point, a peninsula that extends out into Lake Superior. Most of the other families that lived on the point were also relatives. My time with Pauline and her family allowed me to participate in a type of family closeness that I never had growing up in my own family.

Shortly after meeting Pauline, I got orders for reassignment to Da Nang, Viet Nam. I knew it would interrupt my romance with Pauline, but at the same time, I was excited about a new place and adventure. Besides, it was still almost three months before I would be leaving. No one ever liked me for that long.

I also had to go back to San Antonio for combat survival training before heading to Viet Nam. I left for that training in early October of 1967, then home to New York for a week's leave then back to Duluth for processing out. By the time I returned to Duluth, my relationship with Pauline had become serious. I had been seeing some other girls occasionally, but I had stronger feelings for Pauline than any of the others.

Wait a minute. Those last words sound far more mature than I was. It's true that I was genuinely falling in love with Pauline, but I didn't have a clue what true love was all about. I was about as mature as a thirteen-year-old, but somehow my relationship with Pauline continued to grow and no one ever took issue with my immaturity.

I was due to report to Norton AFB, San Bernardino, California for transport to Viet Nan on November twenty-seventh which was the day after Thanksgiving. I spent those last few days with Pauline and her family and remember when I went to sleep Thanksgiving night, Pauline was staring at me and she was still staring at me when I woke up. She said she had watched me sleep the whole night. I remember that being the first time that I thought someone really loved me.

Chapter Seven
Next Stop Viet Nam

On November 27, 1967, I left Duluth for Southern California to be transported to Viet Nam. It was cold and snowing when I left Duluth, but sunny and warm when I arrived in California. I had to take a bus from Los Angeles Airport to Norton AFB in San Bernardino, and I remember enjoying the sights and the sunshine along the way.

When I arrived at Norton AFB, I expected to see a transport plane for the long trip to Viet Nam, but instead, there was a Flying Tiger 707 set up just like a regular passenger plane. We left that evening and stopped in Fairbanks, Alaska to refuel, then in Tokyo for more fuel then we finally arrived early the next morning in Da Nang, Viet Nam.

It was very hot and muggy and totally different than any place I'd ever been. There was a strong smell of burnt jet fuel from all the F-4s coming and going on the taxiways when we got off the plane. I was again assigned mostly to security posts on the flight line guarding F-4 fighter jets, but this time there were a lot more of them and there were a lot more men in my unit. I was assigned the swing shift which was from about 2:00 PM till 10:00 PM. It was constantly loud with F-4s coming and going, there was almost always something going on. It was a lot different than Duluth.

I almost immediately began receiving care packages and tapes from Pauline. We would send two-inch reel to reel audio tapes back and forth as many of the other men did with their girlfriends and families. The tapes normally included personal or romantic messages and some of the newest music. Tapes were the most anticipated mail that we received. Hearing the voices of loved ones helped dull the loneliness.

The first clear memory I have of life in Viet Nam was the night of January 2nd, 1968. I had become such a sound sleeper because of sleeping through Rusty's jam sessions in Duluth, that I didn't wake up for my first rocket attack and I came very close to being killed. My bunk was situated along the front wall of the barracks that was closest to the street and there was an air raid siren not more than thirty or forty feet from it. I slept through the siren and the first twenty or so rockets that landed all around our barracks. Everyone was yelling at me to get under my bed and most of the other men thought I was dead because I didn't respond. I was finally awoken when a rocket landed right across the street and blew the outside wall in on top of me.

Very much stunned by all the refuse that covered me, I rolled out of my bed to get under it but forgot that I was now sleeping in a top bunk rather than the lower bunk that I was accustomed to in Duluth. I had a hard landing on the rough concrete floor and was immediately pulled under the bed by my lower bunkmate Tom.

The attack continued for what seemed like at least another thirty minutes. I don't remember ever being so scared. Every 122mm rocket whistled as it came in and each one sounded like it was going to land in my back pocket. I had my arms through the metal bed frame at the head of the bed and my feet were through the frame at the foot of the bed. The bottom of the frame was about six inches off the ground. Every time I began to hear the whistle of another rocket, my body became so rigid that none of me was touching the floor. After each rocket had landed I would relax and my body would sink back to the floor. They say the first attack is the worst. I guess that's true because I went through about seventy more rocket attacks during my time in Viet Nam and don't ever remember being that scared again.

A few weeks later, the Tet Offensive began which I think was the strongest and most coordinated enemy offensive of the whole war. We didn't know a lot about what was really going on, only what we were told. Most of the army and marine troops had been sent home for Operation Santa Claus a month earlier, so part of our unit was assigned as a blocking force during the Tet offensive. As I remember, there were about twenty-five of us from my security unit that were led by a few marines. Our assignment was to be airdropped into bases that had been overrun by the enemy to reclaim each of the bases. I say airdropped, but to state it more clearly, our C-130 landed at each base and we unloaded ourselves down the rear tailgate ramp as our aircraft taxied down the runway.

I only remember being in one firefight early in the assignment to the blocking force. The rest of the time we spent on the C-130 traveling from base to base. Fortunately, each time we landed, the enemy had already fled. We didn't see much combat, but we were almost constantly on the move. The only sleep we got was on the plane between bases. The offensive lasted about a month, but we were relieved after about ten days.

One of my clearest memories was on our last night, they let us go to the mess hall in Da Nang for a hot meal after ten days of eating cold canned-rations.

It was late evening, maybe as late as midnight. We all had our trays of food and were about to sit down and enjoy this highly anticipated meal when the air raid siren went off. I remember we all scanned the faces of one another and without saying a word we all took our trays and clambered under the tables and ate as though nothing else was going on in the world other than our meal.

I remember taking off my boots that night for the first time in ten days and having to peel my socks off my feet in pieces. I feel very fortunate that wearing the same socks that had gotten wet during the first firefight didn't cause any permanent damage to my feet.

About a month later, I was offered a transfer to a security outpost on Monkey Mountain just outside Da Nang. The unit's objective was to guard a radar facility that directed most of the US aircraft and air strikes in the war. It was considered choice duty because we were so far from the base that we almost never had inspections or visits from superiors. I accepted the assignment and moved up there at the end of February. It was at such a high altitude, that we were in the clouds most of the first few months I was there, so I rarely saw beyond about twenty feet until April.

It was great being so far from everyone, but the humidity from the clouds created a serious problem. We were housed in a wood-framed screened hut and as a result, everything was always damp or downright wet. We were issued electric blankets to keep our beds dry. Which we also found very useful for keeping our M-16s dry when we were off duty which kept their barrels from rusting. The blankets were a big help for our bodies and our rifles, but they also offered a cozy spot for snakes that made themselves at home while the beds were empty.

Occasionally we were able to go to the Airmen's/NCO club for drinks or a meal at the bottom of the mountain where everyone else lived. About once a month they would have music entertainment from the U.S. We also visited the China Beach Exchange, which wasn't too much farther. It was the regional military shopping area. It was huge, and you could purchase just about anything there. Anything from cigarettes and liquor to stereos and jewelry. Unfortunately, leisure transportation was limited, so we spend most of our time at our base at the top of the mountain.

There were about twelve of us who took turns on night posts guarding the perimeter of the radar unit which was situated about one hundred yards from our camp. Six of us would work one night, then the next night the other six would work. We always had a good stock of alcoholic beverages and we drank a lot. There wasn't much else to do during our off time. There were just the twelve of us and our dog Claude. At first, I was not as enthusiastic a drinker as the rest of them which is saying something. To fill some of my time I volunteered at a MARS radio station, which was also on the top of the mountain, where we patched calls via radio back to the U.S. for the service guys in the area. It gave me the opportunity to call Pauline once or twice a week.

Before long, I began catching up with the others on drinking. I had my first experience with marijuana there as well. It must have been very powerful stuff because it almost knocked me out. I didn't try it again for a while, but over time I became a regular user. I really don't know where the stuff came from, but it was always there. When we were off, we were drunk or high. One night one of the guys was so drunk that when he turned his blanket back to go to bed and found a snake, he shot the snake and passed out in his bed without removing the snake. That was the state of most of us when we went to bed.

As I said, we were in the clouds most of the time, but when it cleared up, you could see for miles. We overlooked Da Nang, Da Nang Harbor and all the military installations in the area. It was a breathtaking view. Although I never witnessed it myself, they said that on a real clear night you could see the firefights on the DMZ (Demilitarized Zone) one hundred miles away.

The most significant memory from my time on Monkey Mountain was the night of May 1, 1968. The enemy launched a major attack on all Da Nang that night to commemorate May Day the communist holiday. It was an amazing yet disheartening sight. We had a bird's eye view of everything that was happening and because we had base security radio receivers, we could hear the frantic communications on the base. It was extremely frustrating because we could clearly see the strategies of the enemy as they were being carried out, but had no way to communicate what we saw to the base. We could see the enemy firing mortars and artillery from underground positions long enough to draw a response from a helicopter or gunship, then they would cover that position and blow our aircraft out of the sky from a position just behind the first firing position. I think we counted twenty-seven gunships and choppers that were blown out of the air that night.

In July, as one of the men assigned to the blocking forces during Tet, I was given my choice of bases in Viet Nam for reassignment. I didn't hear until later that we were considered the most experienced combat troops that the Air Force had in the country and they wanted us to be spread out to other bases for an anticipated new enemy offensive. I chose Phan Rang because it had never been hit by rockets. Not necessarily because I was afraid, but I assumed it would be a more relaxed atmosphere. Before I left for Phan Rang, I went to the China Beach Exchange and bought an engagement ring for Pauline and sent it to her.

After arriving in Phan Rang, I enjoyed the extra freedom, privileges, and attention I was given as a seasoned warrior, (I let them believe the press that they had received about our group). But it didn't take long for my new base to start getting rocketed. It seems like half of the seventy attacks I experienced in Viet Nam were in Phan Rang. It was a more relaxed environment though, and my drinking only increased in that more casual environment.

I was assigned the night shift from 9:00 PM until 5:00 AM. When our shift ended, we would typically drink in the barracks until the gates opened to town at 7:00 AM. Then we would go to the "Strip" to drink and party until about noon, then go back to the barracks and sleep till about 5:00 PM. We'd then go to the NCO Club and have supper and drink until it was time to go back to work. I know we got very drunk at the Strip, and even though we probably drank more at the NCO Club I rarely remember being incapacitated for work.

The Strip was an interesting place. It was owned by the base and was a community of about twenty or thirty bars that also served as houses of prostitution where the girls were regularly given checkups for disease and had a special team of base security police. It was a very popular place for most of the men. I guess the base used it as a place to contain the men in a reasonably safe environment. It was quite a place. There were about a half dozen of us who ran together through that whole daily routine and never seemed to waver. I remember but hesitate to list the names for fear they might not want to be identified.

If you are thinking I talk a lot about drinking and partying, it's because that was the biggest part of what we did. For the most part, I was a handful for my supervisors, but when it came to being ready for the enemy when he showed up, I still consider myself to have been very conscientious and dependable especially when faced with regular rocket attacks. There's not that much to talk about concerning those attacks. Most enemy rockets were fired from a considerable distance away and were rarely followed up with a ground attack. The barrage of rockets usually didn't last more twenty or thirty minutes. I don't want to dismiss the attacks as insignificant because there were occasionally people killed and major damage caused, but I think the intention of the enemy was more harassment than anything. It was pretty much always the same routine.

Everyone would take cover while we were receiving incoming rockets. I was already at work at night when most of the attacks occurred, so it was a regular routine for me. When the rockets stopped, we mobilized and posted many of the off-duty security personnel from the barracks to the perimeter of the base. After a period of enemy silence or inactivity, we would gather the men up again and take them back to the barracks. Ground attacks were different, it was the responsibility of those of us on duty to engage the enemy and prohibit their entry into the base, but I can only remember one of those attacks, January 26th, 1969.

There was an event that I witnessed that changed my life to this day. One night I was posted at the main entrance to the base at about ten or eleven in the evening. The lights were mostly out because the traffic in and out of the base was over for the day. While a few of us on duty were talking, we heard a scuffle over by the Vietnamese worker entry point about thirty or forty feet away. We turned on the lights and saw two young Vietnamese men fighting over two pieces of slimy green chicken that they had found in the trash can. The fact that these two men were so desperate for food that they would fight over chicken that I wouldn't even touch, rocked me to my core. To this day, I will not leave a speck of food on my plate at a meal.

In October of 1968, I went on R&R leave for a week to Bangkok, Thailand. This was an event that was planned for months with my friends Gil and Terry. It was a great time for sightseeing, partying and experiencing a different culture. Honestly, I'm too embarrassed to share most of my experiences there, but it was a life-changing vacation.

When we got back from Bangkok, I don't know what got into me, but I began thinking that I wasn't ready for marriage and broke off the engagement with Pauline. I also signed up for another six months in Viet Nam. As I said, I don't know what had gotten into me. One of the perks of extending was a free thirty-day home leave. I left for that home leave in early December and on our approach to the U.S. we were told that our destination airfield, McCord Air

Force Base in Seattle was fogged in and we would have to land at SeaTac Airport in Seattle. We were supposed to receive written leave orders when we arrived at McCord defining the dates of arrival and return and the typical rules and regulations of our leave. But the diversion to Sea-Tac caused confusion and no one from the Air Base was there to meet us with our orders. When we asked what to do, they told us to just return when you think you ought to. That was the wrong thing to tell me because I decided that I ought to come back when I ran out of money.

After leaving Seattle, my first stop was Kansas to see my grandmother that I hadn't seen since before my mother died fourteen years earlier. After two days there, I headed to Duluth to visit with my friend Pat, see my old girlfriend Cindy and get my engagement ring back from Pauline.

I had arranged to stay with Cindy, who I had dated before meeting Pauline. Cindy was a beautiful girl, and I really liked her, but for some reason, we never could seem to establish a solid bond. I was hoping that this trip would strengthen or at least establish a better relationship. The first night seemed to go very well, but it went downhill from there. I think Cindy was looking for more romantic security than I could give her, I was very immature. The next afternoon I planned to go to Pauline's for what I thought would be a friendly goodbye then go out into the country with Pat and cut down a Christmas tree for Cindy.

None of my plans went very well. Pauline ended up throwing me and my friend Pat out of her apartment. I'm sure it was my fault, I think we were probably drunk when we got there. Then it seemed to take us forever to find a tree and when we showed up drunk and far later than planned with what was a scraggly tree, Cindy became furious and she threw us out as well.

I stayed in the barracks that night, and as a result, I was able to re-connect with some old friends that I probably wouldn't have otherwise seen. The best was SSgt Hooks, a guy from Detroit. He was very starched, and a very serious soldier and we had become good friends. When he had first arrived in Duluth and became my supervisor, we were at it constantly. He was always serious, and I wasn't. I was good at what I did when I wanted to be, but when I was off duty, I was off. For some reason, we respected each other and eventually became great friends. While I was there on leave, he was getting ready for assignment with the Rangers in Viet Nam, so I gave him my contact info and hoped to cross paths with him there.

After a few days in Duluth, I headed for New York for the remainder of my leave. I don't remember many details of my stay in New York, but I still remember it being 30 of the best days of my life there. I spent time with friends and family and went to a lot of parties. I reconnected with Linda, a girl that I'd met before leaving for Viet Nam. It wasn't a serious relationship, but she was easy to talk with and fun to be around. I really enjoyed the time I spent with her.

After I'd been on leave for considerably longer than my thirty days, the folks at McCord AFB called my parents looking for me and demanded that I return within forty-eight hours. Leave was over, but I had enjoyed myself so much, I figured it was worth whatever it would cost me in discipline when I got back to the base.

When I arrived at McCord, I was broke and pretty shabby looking. I was grabbed by a colonel as I was walking through the induction center and escorted to the barbershop for a haircut because I hadn't had one since leaving Viet Nam. I told him I didn't have any money, so he paid for it. To my surprise, other than a question about why I didn't come back sooner, there was no reprimand at all. It was a long flight back to Viet Nam, and I slept nearly the whole way.

Back in Phan Rang, I got a few dirty looks and a sarcastic welcome back from one of my supervisors for being gone so long, but other than that my extra days of leave didn't cause a problem.

I came back with a terrible attitude. After having so much fun on leave, the reality of six more months in Viet Nam hit me hard. I especially remember the depression I experienced during the first thirty days back. Eventually, I got settled in and resumed my old partying routine and the time began to pass a little more quickly. I was twenty now and would turn twenty-one a few weeks before processing out to go back to the U.S. for good.

When I got back from leave I was assigned the job of supervising a crew of 25 Vietnamese laborers repairing the perimeter dirt roads. Our task was to dig out trenches caused by the rains draining across the roads. We then installed twelve to twenty-four-inch diameter culverts in the ditches, and then recover the culvert with dirt, creating a smooth road. While the job could sometimes get boring, it was interesting being around the Vietnamese and observing their culture. I learned that they would work harder if I promised to reward them by letting them spend the last thirty minutes of the work day in the base dump rummaging through the trash. I also learned how resilient they were as a people.

One afternoon, one of our pregnant women laborers went into labor about one in the afternoon. There was no way that I could take the whole crew back to the main base for her to deliver her baby, so a few of the women took her out in the bushes and delivered her baby. When they returned about an hour later, she sat in the truck with her new baby until the others finished their last hour of work. The next morning, she was back and worked as if nothing had happened.

As the day of my departure from Vietnam approached, I anxiously began to plan my new life in the US. At age twenty-one I was supposed to gain access to the five thousand dollars that the Navy had put in trust for me upon my mother's death. I ordered a brand new 1969 Pontiac GTO from the factory that I planned to pick up as soon as I got my hands on the money. I had also received my orders for my next assignment to Patrick AFB, in Cocoa Beach, Florida. I don't remember anything specific going through my mind, but I do remember I couldn't wait to start my new life.

About a week before my departure date, bad news struck. I came down with malaria. They told me my departure date would probably have to be delayed, but I begged them to give me a few days to try to shake it before they made any changes to the plans for me. I took the medication they gave me and headed for the Strip to down all the Filipino beer I could find. Someone had told me that it was made with formaldehyde and would kill anything that was ailing you.

Sure enough, after consuming the limit, (all I could drink before I passed out), they carried me back to my bunk and I slept and sweated and sweated and slept for two days. When I came to and had eaten something, I headed to the doctor to be checked out. The doctor couldn't believe it, my fever was gone, and I could process out on schedule. No one believes that story. I don't know how I was cured. I was by no means spiritually inclined, so I can't claim divine intervention, but something healed me, and I was on my way home.

Chapter Eight
Back in the USA

I was finally back in the U.S.A. alive, well, twenty-one years old and about to receive both my five-thousand-dollar trust fund and my new 1969 Pontiac GTO.

It didn't take long for me to get the trust bank book signed over to me, get a cashier's check for three thousand, four hundred and six dollars and catch a plane to Detroit. I had ordered the car through a military purchase program while I was in Vietnam and was ready for pick up at a dealership in Detroit. I arrived in the early afternoon and was on my way back home, driving my new car, before dark. I drove the whole seven hundred miles straight through stopping only for gasoline and to eat. I arrived back at my parent's house in Baldwin, New York in the middle of the night.

The next day I couldn't wait to start showing off my new car. Everybody loved it. It was burgundy with a black vinyl top and interior. I found out later that black interior and no air-conditioning were a big mistake when you're driving in Florida, but for now, I was in New York, basking in all the attention of my friends. I never knew I had so many friends. And oh, I forgot to mention that car was fast! It had three hundred sixty-six horsepower, 400 CID engine and a four-speed floor mounted shift transmission. I had it up to one hundred and sixty miles per hour several times and rarely went anywhere on the freeway under one hundred. I got so many tickets, I can't believe I didn't lose my license.

That leave was like a dream come true. I was popular, my car gave me the self-esteem that I'd been lacking, (at least it seemed that way), and I had money in the bank. I went places I'd never been able to go before, especially in the city. I went to concerts in Central Park, the establishments of St. Marks Place in Greenwich Village and Washington Square. Life was amazing. It didn't take me long to get caught up in the culture of those places. I hadn't done any drugs since the marijuana of Monkey Mountain, but all my New York friends had already moved on to other drugs including LSD or acid as they called it. I tried a half a tab of LSD on the fourth of July and it was a night to remember. We went to the Long Beach boardwalk and rode the Ferris wheel while watching the fireworks over the ocean. It's quite a breathtaking sight when you're sober, but it was beyond description with an acid buzz. Then we decided to drive into the city for a visit to St Marks Place which was the happening place at that time. That was a trip that I'll never forget. One of my friends with me, John, had really gone over the top with drugs. He walked around with good-sized speakers strung over his shoulders while carrying an eight-track tape player and a full-sized car battery to power it. I remember it as if it were yesterday that as we drove through the Queens-Midtown tunnel John was playing Communications Breakdown, (by Led Zeppelin) at full volume. The combination of the acid with the dah dah dah dah dah dah dah dah of that song plus the tunnel lights along the sides of the ceiling which seemed like they were about three feet apart coming at me. It gave me a feeling like my head was exploding. I had flashbacks of that experience repeatedly in the years that followed as a reminder of that night.

After arriving in the city, we spent several hours wandering around the clubs and shops of St Marks Place and then continued to wander around Washington Square. Even as high as I was, I still remember watching all the people that were a lot higher than me as we wandered. Finally, we headed back to Baldwin and arrived about sunrise. Nothing was open, so we stole some coffee cakes that were left in front of the Food Fair supermarket by their delivery truck. We ate our stolen breakfast and went home.

That night I came to the realization that I really liked acid and if I didn't watch myself, I could easily become addicted. Please let me say at this point, that if it sounds like I'm recommending the use of mind-altering drugs, I'm not. I'd been fortunate to have a good experience those few times I tried acid, but I have been with other friends who had become addicted and had many terrible experiences.

While I used drugs to deaden my senses much of the time, I had some sober moments as well. But sobriety presented some of its own problems. Since it was the firecracker season, (4th of July), and I had just returned from twenty months of dodging bullets, I found myself ducking and hitting the dirt on a pretty regular basis. I also had an experience one night that I think I will always remember as the most frustrating moment of my life. I had been on a date with a young lady named Kathy and we had stopped at a coffee shop for a snack before taking her home. The coffee shop was right across the street from the Baldwin fire station and while we were enjoying our conversation, the fire siren went off. I don't know how long the siren continued, but it seemed like an eternity.

If there was anything that I had been conditioned to respond to over the past time in Viet Nam, it was the siren. Upon hearing that siren in the war, it triggered several emergency responses that had become part of me. To sit that close to the siren in the coffee shop and do absolutely nothing was one of the most uncomfortable feelings I'd ever experienced. My whole system shut down and I couldn't continue the conversation until the siren was silenced. I apologized to Kathy and she said she understood, but how could she?

During my leave, we began to hear advertisements on the radio for an event called Woodstock to be held in mid-August. In the beginning, they were talking about the Beatles and the Rolling Stones being there, and how it was going to be the event of the century. As the protests about zoning and local issues arose the big-name groups started dropping out. So instead of being a music experience, it began to be thought of by at least my crowd as being a good opportunity to get high for three days.

One of my friends, parents had a cabin in Woodstock and we began planning for a fun weekend. As the planning went on, I began to think more and more about the effects of an acid filled weekend on my system and began to have second thoughts about going with my friends. That sounds like pretty mature thinking from someone who had a normal maturity level of a thirteen-year-old, but where ever those thoughts came from I count it a blessing because I never saw any of those friends again. I often wonder what would have become of me if I'd gone with them to Woodstock spending four or five straight days continually on drugs.

After writing off the Woodstock concert, I began to think about Pauline and wondered if maybe I'd been too hasty in breaking off our engagement. I ended up calling Pauline, who was now living in Colorado and inviting her to visit me in New York. For some reason, she accepted and arrived in a few days. We fell in love again and decided to get married right away. Being in the Air Force, I had to call my new commander in Florida and get his approval as well as permission to extend my leave a few days. He agreed to both and Pauline and I immediately drove to Duluth to organize an August 2nd wedding.

As planned, I found myself caught up in the excitement of the event and the idea of getting married but couldn't ignore the feeling inside that I wasn't ready to be married. I was barely capable of taking care of my own affairs in a mature manner, let alone taking care of a wife and family. But the momentum of the planning was too overwhelming for me to confront, so I continued along with the flow. As I have said earlier, I loved Pauline's family, and now that I was almost part of the family, they began to make me feel like one of them.

About a week before the wedding, Pauline brought up the fact that most of her things were still in Colorado and she needed to go get them. I agreed, and we bought her plane ticket. I agreed because I saw this as a perfect opportunity to make my break. It was still early enough that wedding plans, for the most part, could be canceled and my family in New York could still cancel their travel plans as well. I would pack all my stuff in the car, drop Pauline at the airport and keep going. What a great plan.

I was such a coward that I couldn't even deal responsibly with a situation that could leave a terrible scar on many people's lives. But I was ready to take the easy way out. Until the air traffic controllers went on strike and Pauline's flight was canceled. I was destined to be a part of the Medlin family. Again, I loved Pauline and her family, but in my moments of clarity which were not that frequent, I knew I wasn't prepared to be a married man.

Two days before the wedding I went down to Minneapolis to visit my friend Pat and pick up my family at the airport. Pat was to be my best man and we had a two-man bachelor party. Basically, we got loaded and drunk. The next morning, we picked up my stepmother, my father and my Aunt Anna at the Minneapolis Airport and drove to Duluth for the ceremony that evening. Pat's sister Carmel also joined us for the trip and the wedding. Carmel was a neat girl. She always seemed so mature, but always positive and always ready to laugh.

Pat and I began drinking as soon as we arrived back in Duluth and I was pretty drunk at the ceremony. The partying went on into the night. It seemed like the Park Point event of the decade. Pauline's mother Mony told me on more than one occasion that the Medlin family was at its best at weddings and funerals. There were probably several hundred people at the wedding and Pauline and I were some of the last ones to leave. Again, my ignorance showed up. No one ever told me that the Bride and Groom were supposed to be the first to leave. We got to the hotel and I passed out. Pauline was devastated, and I think she was beginning to see what she'd gotten herself into. The next day after some goodbyes to the family, we left for Patrick AFB, Cocoa Beach, Florida, a support base for Cape Canaveral and NASA.

Upon arriving, we were treated well and connected with several of the married couples in my unit. One of my supervisors, Art, and his wife, were especially nice to us and we spent most of the first few months doing things with them. When he was transferred, and we moved into our first permanent apartment, we connected with Chip and Linda who lived down the alley a few apartments away. I worked with Chip and we all became very close friends. We would go shopping together, we went to the movies, we went fishing and spent almost all the time together.

I was married now, but I still was a partier at heart. I had acquired the habit of drinking about a quart of Canadian Club daily, but switched to rum later which was more affordable. We had parties every weekend.

Shortly after arriving, we found we had a problem with our pay records. We didn't get paid our full check for nearly three months. I think the problem was that my pay status had changed from single to married. That status change required several changes in how my paycheck was processed. Things from a different pay amount, to a different amount of deductions, to where the check was mailed to. It wasn't a big problem at first because we still had the balance of my trust money, but after going through that, things got tight.

I got a part-time job at the commissary bagging groceries and Pauline got a part-time job as a cocktail waitress at a local nightclub. That club was one of the hottest spots in Cocoa Beach, so it ended up increasing our partying considerably. I also got another very interesting part-time job with ABC Television. One evening I was working the security desk at the base when someone from ABC called asking if we might have someone with a security clearance for Cape Canaveral that would be interested in working part-time as a driver during launches. I told them that I would and got to work the launches of Apollo 12, 13 and 14. It was an amazing experience to be at the press site for the launches and to see all the behind the scenes broadcast activities.

During Apollo 12, I worked as a driver escort for an Italian reporter. It was very interesting, but the best part of that assignment was getting to go to the European correspondent dinners. They took turns cooking for the group of about a half dozen. Each night we would go to a different apartment for a different cuisine. It was some of the best eating I've ever experienced. For Apollo 13 I worked as a driver for some of Jules Bergman's family. He was the science editor for ABC. And for Apollo 14 I was only a fill-in driver because I couldn't get enough time off. But as I said, working that series of launches was a very interesting experience and a lot of fun.

Pauline struggled with my lifestyle, but she tried to make the best of it. I think the differences in our levels of maturity were beginning to surface, but we continued.

As my Air Force separation date of July 12, 1970, approached, I was trying to figure out what I would do when I got out of the Air Force, but before I got too far along in my thinking, Pauline became ill. She was pregnant with our daughter Abbi and began to have seizures. The doctors didn't have answers concerning the cause and recommended that I think about staying in the Air Force until we had her health issues resolved.

I did some research and found that if I extended my enlistment twenty months, I could cross train into another career field and get my choice of bases after training. They offered me the career field of Air Traffic Control, I accepted, and we were headed to Biloxi, Mississippi and another tour of training duty at Keesler Air Force Base. We arrived in July and I began school immediately.

This time I was living off base because I was married and had a very diligent study partner in Pauline. She drilled me every hour I was awake until I knew my lessons thoroughly. I maintained an A test average in school, but once again we had a problem with my pay records getting lost. This time the problem was far more serious. In Florida, we had a financial cushion and we were getting partial pay, but this time we had nothing in the bank and we were receiving nothing. It took them ninety days to solve the problem and by that time we were deep into our credit cards.

With a baby almost due we were really struggling. The struggle took a bigger toll than it normally would because we were still having serious problems in our marriage. As I said earlier, the problems started probably a year earlier. I'm sure the foundation issues were my immaturity, my constant drinking, and occasional drug use. I was never unfaithful during that time, but when I was drunk or high I would get friendlier with other women than I should have.

It caused Pauline to be so jealous and suspicious that I was getting where I just couldn't deal with it. She would call for me at work if I was ten minutes late and she would explode anytime another girl got close to me. It got so bad that I remember being afraid to turn my head when I stopped at a traffic light for fear that there might be a pretty girl there. We ended up separating over it and while she was gone, I met a girl that I became interested in. Unfortunately, even though she looked older than me, I found out that she was five years younger and still in high school. I continued to see her after Pauline returned. I even went to visit her a few times after we moved to Mississippi. I don't know why I kept seeing her. The easy answer is I thought I loved her, but I think I was probably closer to her maturity level than I was to Pauline's.

The birth of Abbi in August gave our marriage a shot of positive adrenaline, but it didn't last long. I'm sure we both wanted to make it work if for no other reason but for the sake of Abbi, but our relationship continued to deteriorate. Finally, in mid-October when Abbi was barely one and a half months old, I drove Pauline and Abbi to the airport in New Orleans and dropped them off to catch a plane for Duluth and I returned to school in Biloxi. I'd destroyed marriage number one.

From then on, my house turned into the official party house for the air traffic control school. I was the only one who lived off base so when the weekends came I had wall to wall people. They partied day and night the entire weekend. Somehow, I was able to finish school maintaining an A average and graduated at the end of November. I was assigned to Webb AFB in Big Spring, West Texas for my next assignment. I reported at my new base the first week of January to begin my career as an Air Traffic Controller.

Chapter Nine
The Rush of Air Traffic Control

When I arrived at Webb AFB in Big Spring, Texas, I also had with me what was left of our Biloxi apartment's furniture. When I unloaded it into my room in the barracks, it was immediately decided that I was going to have to make different living arrangements. I got permission to rent an apartment right outside the main gate of the base and invited a few of the guys I worked with to share the apartment with me. They moved in with me, but they were ordered by our supervisors back to base. It turns out that during the short time I was living in the barracks, my car had been searched by one of the base security agencies on a tip that I was a drug user. They had apparently found a baggie of marijuana that I had forgotten about under my floor mat.

I don't know how long it had been there because I hadn't smoked any marijuana in a while. I was never confronted by anyone about the marijuana, but I was labeled from the beginning of my time in Big Spring as someone to stay away from. I also assume that I was watched very closely for a period until the authorities decided correctly that I was no longer doing drugs. Even though I was never confronted about drugs and no charges were ever filed, the label of "problem child" stayed with me while I was there.

Webb AFB was a training base for fighter pilots. I was excited right from the beginning about becoming an air traffic controller. However, I was assigned to the radar unit and my enthusiasm was quickly dampened by all the memory work involved. I had never been an enthusiastic student at anything in my life, but the challenge of the controller rating process was totally overwhelming.

Not to bore you with too much detail, but in simple terms, in addition to all the worldwide rules and procedures that I'd just learned and memorized in school, there is also the equivalent of a three-quarter inch thick book of specialized information for each individual base or airport that had to be memorized as well. It's called the FAA rating process. As an air traffic controller, even though I was in the Air Force we worked under the direct supervision of the FAA.

The book I'm talking about contained everything about the base or airport you're assigned to including all the other bases or airports in the immediate vicinity. It included all the approaches, radio frequencies, emergency procedures and many, many other things that not only had to be memorized, but memorized so well that you could spout them off as quickly as your name or address. Until you could do that to the satisfaction of the rating supervisors, you cannot work an air traffic controller position without a rated-supervisor on the position with you. It was probably one of the biggest challenges of my young life, but upon being rated, it was probably also the most rewarding. And it wasn't long before my abilities were tested.

On my first full-day on the job as a rated controller, I was working the feeder position when an unexpected weather recall occurred. On training bases, student pilots are not permitted to fly routine training missions during inclement weather, so when bad weather blows in, there's a scramble to get all the student pilots back on the ground. On an average day, we would usually have approximately forty training aircraft up at a time. The feeder position controller has the job of directing the incoming aircraft from approximately forty miles out from the base into the final approach traffic pattern where he would hand them off to the final approach controller.

All air traffic control facilities are purposely over-staffed so that they have sufficient personnel to handle any emergency and our facility was no different. So, there is always several people on standby in a building connected to the facility. In the "Creature Comfort," as we called it at Webb, the standby controllers usually watched TV or studied or played board games. The minute an emergency arises, everyone on standby moves back into the facility to deal with the emergency.

Normally during slow times, a rated controller would be on each position and when a weather recall occurred, the standby controllers would come in and take the assistant position with each of the controllers already in position. On that first day of my rating, the weather recall happened so fast that there was not enough time for me to be replaced by a seasoned controller and the assistant position headset hookup connection was broken, so I was unable to be assisted. In just a few minutes I had about a dozen jets on my screen with more coming. Instructing the pilots over the radio was not that challenging, but the assistant would normally carry some of the load by marking the flight strips and making the handoffs to the GCA (Ground Controlled Approach) or final approach controller.

So, for about thirty minutes I single-handedly did the jobs of two controllers, and I can say I did it professionally, but with probably a half dozen rated controllers standing nervously behind me watching and probably praying. After all, I was the problem child, and I don't think anyone expected me to do as well as I did. They all applauded me when it was over, and I think I was able to shed a lot of my negative reputation that day. To this day, I consider that event and my performance that day to probably be my finest hour.

Social life in Big Spring required a little adjusting. It was a small town where everyone knew each other. The only bars when I first moved there were country western, so if you weren't into that, you hung out at the Wagon Wheel Drive-in. It was a drive up a restaurant with car hops that served primarily burgers, like a Dairy Queen menu. But they had a pizza burger that was incredible. I eventually got a part-time job there because I was kind of bored and it also put me in the center of the action. They did a good business, but most of the town's young people just circled the parking lot to see who they might connect with. I had bought a new 1970 GTO before leaving Biloxi that was a beautiful shade of electric blue with a white vinyl top and everyone loved it. So, whenever I went to the Wagon Wheel I always drew a crowd.

I dated a few girls in Big Spring and really got to like several of them, but there was one that stood out, Debbie. I think she was considered the catch of the girls in town and not to sound conceited, but I think I was the catch of the young men. We dated and broke up several times but ended up moving in together. I think we even broke up a time or two after that, but always got back together. I don't think either of us was ready to be married, but we were getting pressure from her father.

I was still married to Pauline and when he found out about that, he really got upset and pressured Debbie and me to resolve what was an embarrassing situation for him. So, I began divorce proceeding in Florida, where I claimed was my home state, and was awarded a divorce from Pauline on December 22, 1971.

While I was in Big Spring, I was offered a maximum re-enlistment bonus that I just couldn't refuse. It was either ten- or twenty-thousand dollars. I'd never seen that kind of money before, so I grabbed it. We bought Debbie a nice engagement ring and paid cash for a new mobile home. Debbie and I got married in Carlsbad, New Mexico in January of 1972. We were doing well. With the reenlistment, I also got a base of choice reassignment.

We decided on Phoenix, Arizona and Luke AFB. With a lot of enthusiasm, we left Big Spring shortly after we were married, but had a very rocky arrival into Luke AFB. The company that was moving our mobile home called us shortly after our arrival in Phoenix with the news that the tongue had broken off our mobile home in El Paso and had to be repaired. It was going to be costly and take several weeks. A man I was going to be working with at Luke, offered to let us stay with him and his family until our mobile home arrived. I don't remember their names, but they were so nice to us. They let us sleep in their bed while they slept on a fold out couch and they helped us get the home site ready for the arrival of the mobile home. Our home finally arrived, and we settled in.

That turned out to be a terrible move for my career in air traffic control, but it opened some exciting new opportunities. I was assigned to a mobile unit, which was totally different than the normal air traffic control that I was doing in Big Spring. Our job was to be ready to deploy and set up emergency start-up air traffic control facilities in the event of war or emergency. It was a system designed in modules that could be packed up, transported and set up again in a matter of hours.

When we weren't practicing packing and unpacking the equipment at our base, we were practicing directing simulated air traffic on the equipment. Once or twice a year we would do an actual practice deployment to another location in the U.S. It was interesting and challenging at first, but I'd never been one for repetitious routines and quickly began to get bored. Debbie had gotten a job as a teller at one of the banks because she liked to be busy as well. We began drifting apart almost immediately. It was obvious that we were both jealous for each other, but we both wanted our freedom as well. Not a good combination.

One day at the bank, Debbie was approached by a recruiter from one of the multilevel or pyramid companies that were beginning to get popular in those days. I think his pitch was something like, "as pretty as you are, you must have a very ambitious husband." She took the bait and gave him our phone number. He invited me to a very convincing presentation where they showed me how I could make millions of dollars by selling their products and sharing the same opportunity with others. I took the bait as well and immediately began inviting all my friends to join me in this amazing opportunity selling automotive additives.

I may have been naive, unpolished, insecure and codependent, but I wasn't lazy. I saw what I thought to be the opportunity of a lifetime and grabbed it with every bit of strength and tenacity I had. I immediately borrowed the thirty-five hundred dollars to buy a franchise and immediately became one of the top producers. Unfortunately, my new road to prosperity experienced some bumps.

Within a month after I bought my franchise, the state director of the organization held a meeting of the franchisees and told us he had a better opportunity for us and scheduled some training classes. As we learned he had been introduced to Scientology and assumed we would all be equally as receptive as he was. I was furious and was on the phone with the area director in Los Angeles that same day. He shared my fury and made an emergency trip to Phoenix to discuss and plan our next moves. He fired the old state director and asked me if I could run the operation. They had no one ready to take over our states' operation from the parent organization.

So, I quickly figured out that the only options I had, were to try to run the operation or let it fold. I knew I wasn't ready, but I had five people ready to buy franchises and stood to make fifteen thousand dollars. I wasn't about to let that go. The regional director had gotten to know me during my franchise training that he had taught and encouraged me to give it a try. He was quick to point out what an opportunity it was. And all anyone had to do is wave opportunity in my face and I was ready. I knew it wouldn't be easy, but little did I know how hard it was going to be.

Chapter Ten
A New Awakening in Business

Until now all I knew about making money was to be the best at what you do, work hard and work as many hours as possible. Those are all concepts I learned from my father. Those are hard concepts to abandon, but I was about to learn new money-making concepts and new levels of income. But before that happened, I would be learning a lot of other new lessons in the transition.

In the multilevel marketing business, you need three foundational things. You need successful role models, enthusiasm and finally momentum. By the time we got started on our own nearly a month had passed, and we had none of those things. Nor did we have operating capital or a successful looking office to work out of. But the franchisees that decided to continue with me were honest, sincere and most importantly, desperately in need to make their investments pay off.

There were only about seven of us that launched to a new office. We were all new in the business and only one had made any money at all. But as I said, we were committed and desperate for success. I was already in a deep financial hole as were the others, but somehow, we scraped together enough money to rent a dumpy twelve by twelve-foot room to hold our business explanation meetings in downtown Phoenix with holes in the carpeting.

We bought an Earl Nightengale motivational movie to show at our meetings and I bought an old reel-to-reel projector that looked like it came from the 1800's to show the film. If anyone looked at our operation with objective eyes, they could have seen it did not project success, but somehow, we started selling franchises.

Meanwhile, I was going broke personally and had to get another job. So, for about two months, I was working at the air force base in the mornings from seven in the morning until about three in the afternoon. Then I went home and slept for two hours. After my nap, I prepared for and gave business explanation meetings until about nine in the evening. At 10:00 PM I went to my job at a convenience store until six in the morning. Then, I started the routine all over again. I did that for two months sleeping only on weekends. I would put my car in park at traffic lights in case I fell asleep. I would have to stand all the time because every time I'd sit down, I'd fall asleep.

I once fell asleep talking on the phone standing up and leaning against my kitchen wall. I slept in that standing position for nearly three hours. I really don't know how I did it, but after two months we were making enough money that I was able to quit the convenience store.

When I did, I felt like I'd been reborn. The parent company was now giving us ten percent of our monthly sales to run the office and within a few more months we were ready to move to a better location. I was still putting everything I was making back into the business, so my financial situation was not improving. I decided to file for a financial hardship discharge from the Air Force so that I could devote all my efforts to the business and got it in April of 1973. I was finally unfettered and free to pursue my dreams of success with all my heart and all I had.

Our Arizona office continued to grow and as it did, the image and lifestyles of our key leaders had to improve with it. All around the other states, the most successful producers were all driving Porsches, Lincolns, and Cadillacs. The pressure to measure up was tremendous. Even though I was making more and more money, I was not making wise choices in my spending. Rather than paying off my twenty or so credit cards, I began spending the money on expensive dinners and trying to project an image of success. We moved into a new facility which was not beautiful, but it was a lot nicer than where we started. It had a nice reception area, a decent sized meeting room, and two offices. Oh, and no holes in the carpet.

Debbie and I continued to drift farther and farther apart until we finally separated, and she moved to Colorado. I really loved Debbie, but we were so different and didn't share the same enthusiasm for the business. I sold our mobile home and I moved into a big thirteen-room house on Camelback Mountain with Jeff and Jim, our other two most successful producers. The house was amazing. It was four levels, with my room, the master bedroom on the top floor. It overlooked our pool and all the heart of Phoenix. At night, with all the lights of the city, it was a breathtaking view. I had never lived in a place that nice, and I was really beginning to feel successful.

I still wasn't making big money, but I was making more than I'd ever made before. I remember one two-week period when I made twenty-five hundred dollars. There was a night that followed when I just couldn't sleep. Not because of my excitement, but because I was thinking if I lose this position where am I ever going to get a job making this kind of money? We continued to grow, but it seemed like no matter how much money I made, I couldn't put a dent in my debt. My appetite for an extravagant lifestyle was growing faster than my ability to pay for it.

We were traveling to conferences all over the country. And the parent company had sponsored several big-name race car drivers and we regularly traveled to different races to enjoy the benefits that went along with being a sponsor. Life was good. Or at least appeared to be.

We finally moved into offices that overlooked the Black Canyon Freeway and it was beautiful. It was probably three times the size of the previous facility and looked extremely professional. It was a little out of our price range, which turned out to be my demise.

To make ends meet, I began to hold back new distributor investment checks before forwarding the funds to the parent company. I'd use a little of the money for expenses. Then when the next distributor check came in, I would repay the previous distributorship funds back and forward those funds to the company. In simple terms, I was stealing from one distributor to pay another without their knowledge. It worked fine until I had used an entire distributorship investment. Before getting any deeper, I told the parent company what I'd done and because of all that I'd achieved for the company in Arizona, they forgave my trespass.

Unfortunately, they sent another man from Massachusetts to help me run our office, so basically, I lost my position. The man they sent had been successful in the company, but it was obvious from the start he was self-serving, cold-blooded and only interested in making money. We got along for a while, but his style of leadership was totally different than mine. The company had become like a family under my management, but he immediately began to teach by his example to a lot of our leaders to start crowding out the weaker distributors rather than helping them. After a short time, I told the parent company I wanted out and they offered me the opportunity to move to the Los Angeles office and I accepted.

As I prepared to leave for Los Angeles I don't remember exactly what was going through my mind, but looking back from where I am now, I can see how the events of that year and a half had done a lot to change the person I was. I had failed in another marriage, my personal financial credit was ruined, and I was leaving all my belongings except some office furniture, clothing, and a few personal items behind in Phoenix. Those facts would have normally devastated me, but the new things I'd learned about life kept my eyes forward and gave me a new determination about the future. I was constantly reminded by others in the company about how I had turned around a dead operation to be one of the best offices in the company. And the training I had received about how persistence relates to success continues to help me today.

I almost memorized the book, *Think and Grow Rich*, by Napoleon Hill. His primary message was that you've never failed until you quit. I'd never known how many people had failed numerous times before they finally found success. I learned the concept of how hard it is for people to move from one class of society to another, whether it's up or down. I had become accustomed to a life of being my own boss and even though there were several bumps in the road before me, I now believed that I had the intelligence, tenacity and most importantly the belief to become a successful, self-employed businessman. One thing that was still not resolved in my mind, was where did God fit in. With all the teaching about positive mental attitude and whatever the mind of man can conceive and believe, it will achieve, I had pretty much given up God for dead. But something happened at one of my training classes that kept that from happening.

I had come to see Christianity as being for the weak and those who couldn't make it on their own. I was rough on Christians in my training classes, to say the least. But one of the trainees did something one day that rocked my world concerning God. We were on break during one of our training sessions and I was in my office with a few of my most loyal trainees when in walked John Miller. He was a Christian man, and new distributor in the class. He stood in front of my desk and boldly asked the question, "Can you stand up and tell me that if you died today, you would go to heaven?" I was stunned and so were the other men in the room. But instead of giving him a sarcastic disrespectful answer as I normally would have, I said, "John, I really don't care about that right now, it's not an issue."

But the boldness he demonstrated to walk into my office in front of those guys knowing that normally I would have chewed him up spit him out, rocked me to my core. The seeds of his words were buried within me that day and even though it would be several years before there was any visible germination or fruit, they began to grow and take root within me.

Chapter Eleven
California Here I Come

I arrived in Los Angeles, more specifically Marina Del Rey in the autumn of 1974 to a very enthusiastic welcome and a beautiful new apartment. One of the directors from the Los Angeles office named Jack had rented an apartment for himself and me overlooking the marina. It was fully furnished and very nice. He had also set me up in an office within the main business office, which was very nice as well. It didn't take me long to get my office furniture moved into the office and my few personal things into the apartment.

Marina Del Rey took some getting used to. I learned quickly that most of the people that lived there, couldn't afford to be living there. I think most of them were trying to tread water and live the life until they got their break. I didn't feel that I fit that description, but maybe I was one of them too. One of my most memorable experiences took place at a marina nightclub. I asked a girl to dance and she asked to see the balance in my checkbook before she'd give me an answer. I couldn't believe it. I didn't do much dancing while I was there.

Living in the marina was invigorating. I remember waking up in the morning and opening the drapes in my third-floor bedroom to the amazing view of the marina. I remember saying out loud many times, man I'm excited to be living here! Celebrities lived all around us and I would see them everywhere. It seemed like I would see Isaac Hayes every time I would go to the grocery store. Several NFL players used to live in our building. I remember OJ Simpson was riding up on the elevator with me one day on his way to visit another player who lived in our building. I always mixed him up with Gale Sayers. So rather than make a mistake, I asked him, "Are you who I think you are?" He naturally said yes. I later figured out who he was. We lived only about ten blocks from the end of Venice Beach, so I enjoyed a lot of time there as well.

Even though I moved to LA with a new enthusiasm about my career, it was hard to ignore that the parent company and the Los Angeles office were in decline. There was a nationwide campaign by the attorneys general to crack down on multilevel marketing and many of the less-than-honest distributors had scattered. But many of us were still committed to what we were doing and continued to sell franchises. The products were great, and we felt that because we were honest in our dealings, the storm would pass. Within a month or so I had sold two distributorships, but for some reason, it was taking a long time to get my commission checks. It didn't take me long to go through the money that I'd brought with me and I began to get nervous. I still had one remaining credit card that hadn't been canceled, but it was quickly getting maxed.

My roommate Jack hadn't done anything to make money in months, but he was from a quite wealthy family. It was getting so tight that we decided to sell our office furniture and use the money to live on. I let Jack handle the sale, but instead of giving me my share of the money, he decided to keep it for upcoming rent. I came to learn that Jack was a jerk. Had I known him better I never would have moved in with him, but as they say, hindsight is 20/20. I really began to panic after that.

The one credit card I still had was a gas card and that company had a truck stop with a restaurant about a hundred and ten miles away in San Bernardino. I started driving two hundred and twenty miles a day to go eat at the truck stop while living in a high-end apartment in the marina. Something's wrong with that picture. After about a week, that card was canceled as well, and I was in trouble.

There was no food in the apartment, because Jack always ate out or with his parents, so I was about to learn what being hungry meant. I started going into some of the nearby restaurants and stealing crackers off the tables. One day I sold a pint of blood to get a few dollars for food. At the end when my commission check finally arrived, I had gone three days without eating. I think those were some of the last commission checks that went out from the company. I was really feeling bad for the two guys that I sold distributorships to, but there was nothing I could do.

After pigging out upon the receipt of my commission checks I began to try and figure out what my next move would be. I felt like I was rich with the commission money in my pocket, but I'd learned how fast money evaporates in the marina, so I began to look for a job. I got a job as a security guard at a very high-end condo only a few blocks away. I knew it wasn't permanent, but the memory of hunger pains was still fresh in my mind and I was determined that I would never go hungry again. I moved out of the marina apartment and into a smaller apartment in Santa Monica.

There was a lot of creative thinking going on among the distributors of the old company. Several of them who still had money decided to start buying up all the additive products from the abandoned distributorships at a reduced price and selling them. The products were excellent, so I decided to go in with Paul, whose brother I'd known very well as a fellow distributor. We decided to try and sell some of the gas additive products to one of the Orange County post office maintenance departments. We made a small sale to test the gasoline additive and we started making a little money. I continued with my security guard job, so between the two, things were picking up. When it looked like we were about to make a sizable sale, Paul and I decided to get an apartment in Orange County so that we could better serve our customers.

I got a new job as a chemist at a recording tape factory near the new apartment and quit the security job. Paul was several years younger than me and kept pretty much to himself when we weren't working. Just as we were about to make a major sale of additives to the post office, they changed managers and we were out of the additive business. I continued to work the night shift at the factory and started looking for work with a better future. I started selling swimming pools for a while, but that didn't work out.

One day I got a call from one of my friends who had joined a multi-level marketing organization that was selling high-end fashion jewelry through a party plan. They offered me a complimentary distributorship and a title of vice president if I would join them in the venture. I accepted and made Paul a partner in my distributorship. It didn't go very well, and my life started heading south again. I had met a girl from the UK, Sheila, who had a three-year-old daughter named Sammie. Sheila and I hit it off and they moved into the apartment with Paul and me.

That arrangement didn't go well either. After a month, we couldn't pay the apartment rent, so Paul quit the jewelry business and moved back home. Sheila and I continued with it and made a little money, but we ran the business from a pay by the week hotel in Santa Ana. Then, I got fired from the factory for being late one night. I was pretty much at the bottom again.

When things got so thin that we were about to be on the street, I got a job as an assistant manager at a pizza restaurant in Fountain Valley. After a month or so I had enough money to move into a house with one of the part-time bartenders at the restaurant. Sheila and Sammie moved in with a friend of Sheila's.

My relationship with Sheila was fading, but I loved Sammie like she was my own daughter. In our short time together, we had formed a very strong bond. I probably would have continued my relationship with Sammie if Sheila had not used my relationship with Sammie to force me to spend time with her. It was sad. I would think regularly about my daughter Abbi's life and what was going on with her. I had totally broken contact with her and her mother because I was devastated every time I had to tell Pauline that I wasn't able to help her. It made me feel like a terrible failure. That wasn't far from the truth, but I still hated admitting it. I think Sammie gave me a fresh start to love.

After several months at the pizza restaurant, they fired the manager and asked me to take his position. I accepted, and I finally began to feel like stability might be creeping into my life. I became friends with Donna one of our student employees. She was about twenty-one and a university student studying to become a nurse. She and her family only lived a few blocks from the restaurant, so it was very convenient to drop in for visits with her and her family.

As our friendship grew my friendship with her family grew as well. It was a large, strong Catholic family. She was the oldest of four girls and two boys. It was such a loving family, like Pauline's family. I envied people from close, loving families. We started doing projects together. Her mother, Fran was an amazing woman, she accepted me as I was, and very few people did that. Her unconditional acceptance made a lasting impression on me. Fran and I reupholstered one of their chairs together, and Donna and I planted a vegetable garden together at my house. On weekends Donna and I used to go exploring up through Topanga Canyon and Malibu to visit the shops, weekend theaters and whatever else we came across. Sometimes we took her brothers and sisters. We spent a lot of time together.

I'd never been in a relationship like that before. Females had been either my girlfriends or my friends but had never been both. I don't think either of us really started out the friendship with romantic intentions, but before long we were headed in that direction. An internal conflict arose in me as I began to realize that I was no good for Donna. Besides being about six years older than her, our lives were headed in totally different directions. As things began to improve my personal finances, I began going out to clubs again at night. I didn't want to expose her to that life, but I wasn't ready to give it up either.

I don't remember ever caring whether I was good for someone, before that, I had always thought about my own needs first. Now, I wasn't sure what to do.

I became friends with an assistant manager of a Mexican restaurant and nightclub called The Red Onion that I went to on weekends. I had shared with him that I had always wanted to learn how to be a bartender and when he was promoted to manager of a new Red Onion in Anaheim, he offered me a part-time job as a bartender trainee, and I took it. I started out part-time, but within a few weeks, they asked me to go on a full-time schedule. The money wasn't as good as my manager's position at the pizza restaurant, but I supplemented my income by using my GI Bill education benefits and started attending college part-time as well.

Just before I left the pizza restaurant, I received divorce papers from Debbie. It was a surprise, but I took it in stride as I moved on to my new career in bartending. I knew I didn't want to be a bartender forever, but I saw it as an opportunity to be in the middle of the lifestyle I wanted to be in while I decided what would be my long-term direction in life.

I started taking real estate classes at college to see if I could get my real estate license, but I took the licensing test twice and missed passing both times by three questions. The next semester I decided to take some business classes to see where that might lead. I wasn't a very serious student. I guess I might have been if I'd found something that interested me, but for now, I was more interested in getting my monthly GI Bill check.

I met another girl, Janet, one weekend at a club. She was married, but we really connected. She told me she was separated, but I later learned that she really wasn't. It was even stickier than that. She was married to a lawyer that worked for her father's law firm. Had I known that right off, I probably would have steered clear, but by the time I found out, I had seriously fallen for her. In late 1975 we got an apartment together in Anaheim, which was closer to her family in the Pasadena area, and closer to my work at the Red Onion.

The move to Anaheim put distance between Donna and me. We never officially broke up, I don't think friends do that. We were still friends, but we didn't spend much time together anymore. I don't remember ever making any conscious decisions about our relationship, but in hindsight, I think God did. Just as the incident with John Miller had affected me in my thoughts about God, Donna, her mother Francis and their family impacted my consciousness about God even more. The unconditional love that her family had demonstrated for me and for each other was something that God would replay over and over in my mind as He worked his miracle of salvation within me. Donna became my standard for the perfect woman and perfect relationship.

After working as a bartender trainee for about six months, opportunity came for another visit. I was working with a professional bartender named Vic at the Red Onion, and he was not only a good bartender but a good teacher. We became friends at work and seemed to work very well as a team. A new club was opening in Irvine called the Foxhunter and Vic had been hired as one of the new bartenders there. Vic recommended me as a part-time fill-in bartender and they called me within a few weeks of opening. I started working weekends at the Foxhunter while working weekdays at the Red Onion in Anaheim. When you add in an almost full load of college classes, my time was pretty much booked.

By Christmas, I was asked to work full time at the Foxhunter and I gladly accepted. It was quickly becoming the place to be in the area and the money was better than anything I'd received since moving to California. I was finally getting back on my feet.

Things were kind of up and down with Janet. When her husband and family found out about our relationship, she got a lot of pressure from them to end it. We cut way back on seeing each other, but she continued to break away regularly to see me. In hindsight, I think her relationship with me was her act of rebellion with her family. She was very close to her family, but I got the impression that they were very controlling.

In between visits with Janet, I was beginning to have opportunities with a few other women. As I write this I'm asking myself how seriously interested could I really have been about Janet? In retrospect, I don't think it was a question of being serious, as much as it was an issue of her never convincing me that our relationship was going to be permanent. She would move in with me for a few days, then she'd move back home with her parents. She did that several times.

Meanwhile, I was beginning to come out of my shell of insecurity at the Foxhunter. It had become one of the hottest spots in Southern California and I was becoming an excellent bartender. I was stunned by how many women were making advances toward me. It happened almost every night. Honestly, I thought I'd died and gone to heaven. By February of 1976, I had received two very interesting offers for positions at other clubs. The parent company of the Foxhunter asked me if I would be interested in moving to Houston, Texas to open another Foxhunter there. I also had an offer from a company that had a restaurant/club in Newport Beach and another one in Aspen, Colorado. They offered to let me work the summers in Newport Beach and the ski season in Aspen. What a decision to have to make.

I didn't know much about Houston, but I think the deciding factor proved to be that the thought of spending summers at the beach and winters on the slopes scared me. My first thought was that it was a routine that might lull me into a lifestyle that would go nowhere. That sounds like a very career minded thought and it was. While I was thoroughly enjoying my life as a bartender, I always realized that it wouldn't last forever and eventually I would need to put partying behind me and pursue a more permanent career. So, I decided to go to Houston.

I told Janet of my decision to go to Houston and surprisingly, she said she would move there with me. I had gotten thick with another girl, Pam, who I liked very much. I still wasn't sure about Janet, so I never officially ended the relationship with Pam when I moved. I told her I'd be in touch, but she never returned my calls. I think she found out about Janet.

In April, I loaded up the car and a U-Haul trailer and was Houston bound, not having any idea what that city had in store for me!

Chapter Twelve
Houston Bound

I arrived in Houston the fifteenth of April, 1976. I had been told before leaving California that the new Foxhunter would be opening the first of May. It was quite a surprise when I walked into the club in mid-April and found it still in the early stages of construction. Although I was starting to get back on my feet financially, that only meant that I could probably sustain myself for a few weeks of transition, but not for a couple of months before the club would open.

Steve, the manager of the club was already there doing some of the hiring and training of the new employees. He had also found me an apartment that was ready to move into when I got there. He had been the assistant manager in Irvine, so we knew each other pretty well. Steve and I had a unique relationship. We respected each other, that was obvious, but we had a difficult time connecting as friends.

After getting approval from the California office, Steve offered to hire me to work on the construction crew and help with the training of employees. My position rapidly expanded to supervising a lot of the construction and helping with some of the practical design in the work areas of the club. There was even a several weeks period, just before opening that I was sleeping at the club to serve as security before the permanent alarm system could be installed. That place was my life for the five weeks before opening. I spent so much time there and put so much of myself into it, it almost seemed like it was my club.

I had a spot on the second floor where I could stand and see almost the entire club. In the daytime during construction, I could go to that spot and watch all the workers and gage our construction progress. At night I could stand there and see the lights and activity of Houston around us through the north wall of the club which was entirely smoked glass. After we opened, I used to go and stand there and watch the activity of the club and try to figure out what was being said by the five hundred or so people as I watched them talk and drink and dance.

The Friday night before we opened, I was in the club alone and standing at my spot at about ten o'clock watching the people across the street going into Daddy's Money, the club which had been Houston's hot spot up until now. It was surreal to watch those people from the quiet and emptiness of our building and thinking that many of those same people would be crowding into the Foxhunter in a few nights.

We worked, what seemed like night and day preparing the club for a Sunday press party to show off the new hot spot. The day before we opened I got into it with one of the junior partners of the parent company. He ordered sliding doors be welded on the top of the ice bins in all the bartenders' stations to keep the ice from melting. I tried to explain to him that he would lose more money by impeding the work of the bartenders with the doors than he would ever save by keeping the ice from melting. He would not acknowledge that I was right, so after he left that afternoon, I went around and chiseled all the stainless-steel doors off all eight bartenders' stations. He was furious.

Because of this incident, whatever position I had agreed to at the new club was gone. I was supposed to be bar manager. I agreed to stay as a bartender if our original agreement that I could drink while I worked stayed in place, He agreed, and I stayed on as a bartender, but all my authority and responsibility was gone. As it turns out, he did me a big favor. I had helped train all the bartenders and cocktail waitresses as well as the new assistant managers so they all looked at me as the authority. And because I was one of the best bartenders, I got all the best shifts. I was also the only employee allowed to drink while working and had no management responsibility. In my eyes, life had gone from being good to better.

We finally opened, and the club was far more successful than anyone had dreamed. We opened at four in the afternoon and by six o'clock we had a waiting line to get in. It was the first club in

Houston that catered to an upper-class clientele at a time when the oil industry was booming.

We were all amazed at the eccentricities that became normal events of working there. It wasn't uncommon for the bartenders and cocktail waitresses to make four or five hundred dollars a night in tips. Nor was it uncommon to get outrageous offers from the customers. I was offered five hundred dollars for my bartender's shirt one night by a man trying to impress his girlfriend. A CEO of one of the biggest Japanese electronics companies made me an amazing offer to build him a club just like the Foxhunter in San Francisco. Another man named Gene made me a lucrative offer to join him in his bill collection business, an offer which I eventually accepted.

I used to take breaks and walk outside like I was checking the parking lot, but I really went out there to listen to offers the people standing in line would make me to get them into the club. Because of my position, it seemed like everyone wanted to be my friend or my girlfriend. I quickly went from being a shy guy with no self-esteem to being "Lance Romance." There would always be several girls that waited around till closing to see if I'd take them out after work. We worked extremely hard during club hours, but there was a party almost every night after work. And there were offers from the customers, so they'd be invited to the parties. I can't remember how many times I played golf at Houston area country clubs because I allowed an oil executive to be my guest at a party.

I typically worked from 8:00 in the evening until 1:30 in the morning. Then I would go out and party till about 6:00 AM. I would go home, nap for a few hours, then play golf or tennis till early afternoon, take another nap then go back to work at the club. I did that usually Tuesday through Saturday. As I said we worked hard at the club, and by Sunday morning I was usually so tired, I slept till three or four in the afternoon. Life had seemed to become better than a dream.

I even got to reconnect with my daughter Abbi, who was now seven. She came to Houston and visited with me for a few weeks. My life revolved totally around her while she was there. I got to teach her to swim and we took a short vacation to Tennessee to visit the farm where I spent my summers as a child and all my relatives there. It was a great time.

I had everything that I thought would make me happy. But despite having it all, after about a year of living that lifestyle, I began to have feelings of what seemed like loneliness or emptiness during the times I was alone and away from the parties. Those feelings became more and more persistent as time went on. I would sometimes go up to my spot on the second floor of the club and just gaze at the goings on around me, and I began to wonder what life was all about. I don't remember ever having raised that question before.

Then one night I had a moment of clarity. A moment when my world stopped and demanded some answers. I was standing on my spot, gazing at the club activity. It was only about 9:00 PM, but I was planning to take off early. I was thinking it was too early to go home so I would scoop up one of the girls and we'd go out. It never crossed my mind that whoever I chose would ever say no. Nobody ever said no to me anymore. As I was taking an inventory of my options, I remember thinking, *"I really don't want to go out with anyone,"* followed by the thought, *"I have everything I ever thought would make me happy, so why do I feel so empty inside?"* At that point, I left the club and I remember driving down San Felipe Street back to my apartment at ninety miles an hour bouncing off the curbs on each side of the four-lane street. It was a miracle that I didn't flip my car due to my erratic steering. I wasn't drunk, I don't think I'd had anything to drink, but I was totally frustrated that my life had come to what seemed like a dead end. That night began a journey of about a year and a half of questions and searching for answers.

Chapter Thirteen
What's Life All About Anyway?

The experience I had that night set a lot of things in motion and reminded me of some things that had happened back in California. I had never been what I would consider a spiritual person. As a matter of fact, because of teaching positive mental attitude concepts back in the multilevel marketing days, I wasn't sure I even believed in God.

While I was still in California I'd gone to see the movie *The Exorcist* with Donna and it apparently had a strange and powerful effect on me. I remember one night not too long after I'd seen the movie, I woke up flopping in my bed like I'd seen Linda Blair doing in the movie when she was possessed. Only my bed wasn't moving, only me. Even stranger was that I was sleeping next to Sheila and she never woke up. I mean I was flopping up and down for what seemed like as much as a foot in the air. I can still remember it so clearly, that it couldn't have been a dream. I've often wondered in hindsight, if maybe a demon had entered me that night. Demon or not, I can see that my life was taking a definite spiritual turn.

It's hard to remember the exact chronology of all that happened over the next year and a half. I was doing a lot of drugs and I began changing addresses quite a bit so it's difficult to sort out. I remember waking up in the middle of the night after my moment of clarity at the Foxhunter to what I remember to be a light and a voice of authority in my room saying, "You are God!" Again, it was so clear, I don't think it was a dream.

From that point on I began to have visions of a plan for developing a systematic society that reorganized the world. I saw things that hadn't yet been invented, like a system of everyone in the world having a number and an account in a central computer where every financial transaction in the world had to go through.

Don't forget this is 1977, computerization and networking were just getting started, these were truly revolutionary dreams. There were sensors everywhere, at every entry point in every building, store, and house so that you could be located at any time. There was a system of payment for everything through the central computer. You could pay for gas at the pump, something that we take for granted today, but was not yet in practice at that time. There was no more debt or crime because the system made it impossible.

I saw cities that were totally planned and operated to the highest level of efficiency. All the plans and systems were not intended to control people, but to help them make the best of every area of life and to help eliminate crime. In today's world, many of these things are common, but in 1977 they were unheard of. All these visions happened over a period of probably about a year.

As they were happening, I really wasn't sure what all these things meant, but while I was trying to figure it out, I began making career changes. I worked for a while with Gene, who had invited me to come and work with him in his collection business. It wasn't an arm breaking collection business. It was based on a series of computer-generated letters to collect bad checks and debts. People were a lot more honest then and the system worked well. Gene had some impressive clients. There were a major airline and several well-known retail stores that used the system effectively.

At the time, Janet was still pressuring me to move back to California, so I came up with the idea of opening a California office for Gene's company. I quit the Foxhunter and made a temporary move back to California to try my idea. Rather than starting small, I went after some of the big airlines headquartered in California. Those kinds of accounts don't get opened overnight so it didn't take long for me to get discouraged and give up.

While I was there, Janet's family made Janet and me an offer to let me work at one of their restaurants with the opportunity to take it over if I did well. They even offered to build us a house in Palm Springs if we would only move back to California. Their offers were very tempting because I really thought Janet was a great girl who I felt I was very compatible with, but I kept thinking that if I went to work for her family, I would be under their thumb. So, I went back to Houston with a very unhappy Janet. Within what seemed like only a few days she was back in California.

After I returned to Houston, a former co-worker named Penn, who I'd worked with at the Foxhunter contacted me and asked me if I wanted to work at his family's new restaurant that was opening in Clear Lake City near NASA. I needed a job, so I accepted. I worked there for a few months as an assistant manager and bartender. The restaurant didn't really take off as they'd expected so they let me go and I moved back to Houston. Janet called me about that time to tell me she wasn't coming back, I think we both knew that a permanent relationship was not going to happen, so we parted company over the phone as friends. At least I think it was as friends.

Back in Houston, I moved in with Debbie, but she was just a friend. She was a customer from the Foxhunter and was also friends with another girl I had dated, Diane. I also joined back up with Gene at the collection company. Gene and I had become good friends. We worked well together and at the end of each day, we'd go out to happy hour, usually at the Foxhunter and we'd drink on the company credit card. His company was beginning to struggle, primarily because of changing times. I didn't make much money there, but the company credit card never seemed to go dry for happy hours.

I had started dating Lorna while I was working in Clear Lake. I was spending Christmas weekend at her house with her and her housemates when another strange thing happened. I'd fallen asleep on the living room floor in front of the TV on Christmas Eve. Christmas was on a Sunday that year and when I woke up and turned on the TV, Evangelist Oral Roberts was on. He had a strange message about being told by God that a man would come into being before the end of that year, 1977, that would change the world. That freaked me out because, for some reason, I felt like he was talking about me. With my search for the meaning of life with, the voice I had heard in my room, my visions about reorganizing the world, and now the message from Oral Roberts, I was becoming consumed and bewildered by what was happening,

The next thing that happened was one Sunday morning early in January when I woke up with an undeniable urge to find a black church, a church whose membership was African-American. So, in surrender to the urge, I got up and drove through Houston's Third Ward until I found the one I felt I was looking for. In those days, I slept late, so when I found the church, the services were already over and the building was a locked up. So, I copied the pastor's name and phone number off the signboard and went home.

The moment of clarity I'd had at the Foxhunter had given me the impression that if I gave of myself to others, it might help fill the emptiness that I was feeling. So, when I had the urge to find a black church, I think I figured that maybe helping inner city people might be an opportunity to give of myself.

As I said earlier, I was doing a lot of drugs at that time and it's hard to recall how one event led to another, but it seemed like for some reason, my life was beginning to take a definitely different direction. The next day I called the pastor of the third ward church, His name was Dr. Weaver. He was maybe seventy or so years old. I shared with him the things that had been happening. He asked me some questions and told me that he had turned over most of his responsibilities within his group of affiliated churches to two younger pastors and asked me to contact them. I was amazed at how intently Dr. Weaver listened to me. I halfway expected him to tell me I was nuts. I called the two pastors that Dr. Weaver suggested, Reverend Morrison and Reverend Gage and set up separate meetings with each of them.

By the time of the meetings, I had started combining some of my visions and came up with what I thought was a attractive plan for an organization that could help inner-city people. People could become members of an organization that would charge a fee for membership. The fees would be pooled and used to form businesses that would employ and utilize the talents of the members.

The concept in its simplest form was that while the inner-city people were individually poor, as a group they had considerable financial capability. Both pastors liked the idea and asked me to begin explaining and promoting the idea in their churches and in the other churches that they were affiliated with. My first few presentations went well and speaking opportunities became more and more frequent.

Meanwhile, I was still working at the collection company and had pretty much taken over the leadership. We had hired several of the bartenders and cocktail waitresses from the Foxhunter and offered to let them share in the profits of the company if they would help us build our client list. I think we all thoroughly enjoyed working together in a professional setting after working in the club.

As a result, the company started growing. About that time, I connected with Jenny. She was a flight attendant and we had met the year before. We really seemed to connect at the time, but she was engaged, so we never dated. When I saw her again in February, the first thing I asked was whether she had gotten married. She said no, and we went out a few days later. I moved in with her after the first date and we became a couple.

By spring, my speaking appointments at the black churches had increased from one or two a week to nearly every night. I remember being both overwhelmed and overcome by the demands and prospects of what was happening. I had a pocket tape recorder and I would tape my presentations on as I spoke and then come home and listen to them with my friends. My ego was beginning to grow.

As the opportunities to speak increased my involvement in the collection company decreased. I began spending my mornings and afternoons sitting on our apartment's enclosed eight by ten patio smoking pot and formulating plans and directions for our new inner-city organization.

We were gaining momentum and I began getting invitations from the black student organizations at the local colleges and university to share the plan. I began meeting regularly with students, teachers, and professors from around the Houston area. I was beginning to truly believe that I was on a mission to reorganize the world starting with the inner city of Houston. If you can believe this, one morning I called the office of the president of the Baylor School of Medicine and told the receptionist that answered, I was going to put the world back together and if they wanted to observe me doing it, they were welcome. After what seemed like a lengthy silence on the other end of the phone, I think she told me she would have to get back with me. I can't stop laughing as I write this thinking of what that girl must have thought. Anyhow, at the time, I was serious as a heart attack.

Jenny and I got married on September 2nd. I continued to meet, speak and strategize the idea of the organization with several black community members until late in the fall when my whole life hit a brick wall.

In November of 1978, I gathered all of my most enthusiastic leaders in promoting the idea of the organization and said we have been talking about this for a number of months, but we have not asked for any commitments to be a part of it. We felt like we had as many as twenty-five hundred people ready to sign up, but that was just a consensus guess. I told them that I felt it was time to stop talking and start moving forward with the idea. I told the leaders that for the next week I will stop promoting and it was up to them to get commitment cards from the people so that we could see what we had to work with and get started with the program.

For the next week, I planned to stay at home, kick back and wait and see how many followers we had. I say "followers," because that's exactly what I thought. I had put myself on a pedestal and considered myself a savior. I had also begun to consider myself above the rules that would apply to everyone else. There was no way that I could have even imagined what would happen during my planned week of R&R.

I rarely watched TV in those days, but on Tuesday night of that week, I watched a documentary on Jim Jones and the Jonestown Massacre. I couldn't believe how much I could relate to this guy, and it began to open my eyes to the reality of what I was doing. The next night I watched a movie entitled, *The Ten Last Days of Hitler*. Shockingly, I could relate to him as well.

Both men seemed to start out with good intentions and as their success and power grew, they turned into egotistical madmen. As much as the first movie opened my eyes, the second movie scared me to the point of wanting to find a place to hide until I could figure this all out.

During the previous months of promoting the organization, I'd had several people make comments along the lines of, *sounds like you're the Antichrist.* I had no idea what they were talking about, so I blew off their comments, but now I was determined to find out exactly what that meant. At that time, I knew nothing about the Bible except some things that I learned in Vacation Bible School as a kid in Tennessee. I don't even think I understood the concept of Jesus. So, the Antichrist was something totally foreign to me. But the more I investigated, and the more I learned, the more scared I got. As I learned more and more about the antichrist, I started praying on my knees for hours at a time, repeating the same plea over and over. *God, please don't let me be the antichrist, please don't let me be the antichrist!*

As I panicked and prayed I began recalling some things that happened during my presentations at the churches. When I first began making presentations, they would put me at the beginning of the services. I would speak, then I would leave, and they would continue with their worship services. As time went on they started asking me to speak at the end of the services which meant that unless I wanted to insult them, I had to sit through the entire church service. That wasn't so bad when it was only once or twice a week, but when I started speaking almost every night, I started getting religion. There were several times as I listened to Bible messages that I felt were talking directly to me. I pondered that a lot. I used to wonder, how could they know that about me? It happened most of the time when Reverend Morrison was the speaker.

Those recollections prompted me to start visiting with Reverend Morrison on a regular basis in hopes that he could help me understand what was happening in my life. I put all my speaking engagements on hold indefinitely and began attending Reverend Morrison's church as a seeker rather than a speaker. Within only a few weeks, I was at his church, True Light Missionary Baptist Church, and during the invitation of a Sunday morning message, I found myself in the front of the church receiving Christ as savior. I don't remember getting out of my seat or walking down the aisle, but there I was in front of the church membership as a new believer. I followed through and was baptized on the first Sunday of January 1979.

Chapter Fourteen
Saved and on a New Journey

I don't remember getting out of my seat or walking down the aisle or making a conscious decision to do either. I was totally dumbfounded by the whole thing. I remember saying to Reverend Morrison in front of the church, that I really didn't understand what just happened, but I was going to do my best to try and understand. Here I was, a man that not too long ago had ridiculed Christians in my classes and wasn't sure that I even believed in God, now accepting Jesus Christ as my Savior. I was blown away by the whole idea. I was a person that didn't believe anything that I couldn't see, touch or be proven and I had made a profession of faith.

I couldn't deny that there was something going on inside me. I remember describing my life at that time as having one end of a rope tied around my neck and the other end tied to the bumper of a car and being dragged behind the car. I hated every minute of the transition process, but I couldn't and wouldn't let go.

I started meeting with Reverend Morrison even more frequently and started reading the Bible but kept a very low profile about it. I had a lot of people with whom I'd shared my vision for the inner city, and they wanted answers. A lot of them had helped with the development of the plans and were waiting for updates and direction, and I had none. I didn't know how to tell them that I'd discovered I was on a wrong path and I was too embarrassed to tell them that I was during a spiritual awakening. I didn't know what to tell anyone, so I pretty much went into hiding, trying to figure it all out.

Everyone at the True Light church was cheering me on in my new faith and encouraging me to get involved there with them at the church. The only thing that I saw that I could help with was with the youth. True Light was in northeast Houston in a pretty tough neighborhood. The church had a facility that was extremely underused. It was a lot bigger than what they needed for their level of ministry activities, and I saw so many things that they could do to utilize some of the extra space. I was not yet seeing things through spiritual eyes, so most of the suggestions I made for programs, activities, and space usage were not necessarily of a spiritual nature.

It was easy for even me to see that many of the church kids were getting involved with the bad kids from the neighborhood because the church didn't offer much for them. We started youth activities several nights a week and the kids really got excited. We had a bowling night, a movie night and several other activities.

While, I was involved with True Light and searching spiritually, the reality of my responsibilities as a husband and father were starting to become a serious issue. Jenny had been very patient with me as I went through the metamorphosis of my new spiritual awakening. When she met me, I was still riding the wave of popularity from the Foxhunter. Then, she was there as I transitioned to orchestrator of the Collection company reorganization and after that into a cult organizer and now to a man searching for spiritual truth. She was pretty much supporting us financially through it all, but she was now pregnant, and her patience was wearing thin. The collection company had moved on without me and I really didn't want to go back to bartending because of my new spiritual views, but I had to do something to earn money.

I got a call from a friend who was putting together a new club in downtown Houston called Mumm's and asked if I wanted to be a bartender. Because of my finances, I had to accept, so I was back to the bar business. I swore to myself that it was only temporary, and I began looking into other things as well. I even went to a career advisor and was tested to see what my natural abilities were. I learned that I was a natural promoter and idea developer. That was very interesting news, but there's a lot of competition for positions that employ those skills and those positions require a strong resume. So, to break in and use those talents, you needed a place to intern for very little money to get started. I needed to make more than an entry-level wage, so I stuck with bartending. I left Mumm's after a few months and went to a restaurant club called Spiro's.

In July of 1979, Jenny gave birth to our daughter Lindsey. It was an amazing experience to be involved with the birth. I loved Jenny more than I'd ever loved anyone, but between her postpartum depression and my multitude of career changes, we were growing farther and farther apart. I wasn't much help with her depression because I still hadn't figured out what my fundamental issues were.

The spiritual changes I was going through had turned my whole world upside down. I had always been a good worker and I wasn't lazy, but I wasn't going to be much good to anyone until I learned which way was up. I kept the job at Spiro's even though I hated it, and by the day of our first anniversary, in September, Jenny and I split up.

Something amazing happened that day as we were moving out of our apartment. We had an argument in the middle of the move and Jenny picked up a CMU block, (concrete block), and threw it at the rear windshield of my car. It only took a second, but a lot happened during that second. I didn't have insurance on the car, and as she raised the block over her head to throw it, a picture flashed in my mind of a huge hole in the window. At that point, I had started to get more and more spiritual, but without time to pray, I just shouted *Jesus!* As the block hit the window it crumbled into sand. It stunned us both. Jenny got pale and I was elated. I started seeing what I considered to be more and more miracles in my life after that event.

Jenny moved in with her mother and I moved in with a friend named Glenn. Glenn had worked with me at the Foxhunter and had pretty much taken over the collection company. I moved one of my couches into the dining room of Glenn's apartment and that was my bed for the next few months. I helped Jenny move back to Atlanta the next month while I was still doing everything I knew to try and reconcile the marriage. Shortly after Jenny moved back to Atlanta, I was hired by an oilfield equipment company as a draftsman, I was only making a few dollars over minimum wage, but at least I was out of the bar business. I made one or two trips to Atlanta to visit

Jenny and Lindsey, but she had pretty much made up her mind that she was filing for divorce.

After Jenny and I had separated, I crossed paths again with Debbie, the girl I had shared an apartment with a few years earlier. She had become a Christian too, and we started hanging out together. She was going to a Southern Baptist church and started inviting me to singles gatherings at her church. I had continued my involvement with True Light, but their theology did not go deep enough for me. I wasn't learning much there that I didn't already learn in my own studies. Debbie and her friends introduced me to Christian radio, Christian bookstores and other sources of Bible knowledge.

I became like a sponge soaking up spiritual learning from everywhere. I listened to the Bible teachers on Christian radio and started attending Bible studies all over town. I was really starting to grow spiritually. I grew to the point where I felt that I had to start taking some major steps of faith to see if what I was learning was true.

Jenny did file for divorce and it was final in January of 1980. When that happened, I decided that it was time to take a total leap of faith. I quit my drafting job and got a paper route. I also started as a volunteer at a ministry called *The Old Time Religion Hour*. They were in the process of trying to obtain a television operating license and needed someone to help promote their efforts. They told me they would pay me as they were able. Basically, I was a volunteer by faith. But that's what I wanted, something that taught me to become totally dependent on God. I figured that I could make enough to pay my child support for Lindsey through my paper route, but I would be in the thick of ministry work to further my spiritual growth.

Debbie invited me to go with her church singles group on a weekend retreat to a deer lease in the Texas hill country. I went for the new experience, and there I met a woman named Dina. She had been divorced three times and had two sons, Mark who was eleven and Robert who was seven. I really had no intention of getting involved with anyone until I could make some sense out of my life and Dina said the same thing, but we connected instantly and by the time we got back to Houston a few days later, we were on the road to becoming a couple. We went out on a few dates but by March I was spending nights at her house.

I had finally reached a point in my spiritual journey that I was beginning to have a real relationship with God, but I didn't yet have the self-discipline to control the events of my relationship with Dina. I was having supernatural experiences with God, but I was constantly being pulled into things in our relationship that we should not have been doing. Dina's mother began calling me, telling me what a bad influence I was on her daughter and grandsons. Although I had overcome my insecurity around women, my self-discipline in matters of confrontation was still with me. I knew I needed to end my relationship with Dina or at least stop sleeping at her house, but I didn't have the strength to do either.

One morning when I was in prayer, God told me he would use me in a mighty way if I stayed single and pure. Because of my fear of confrontation, I couldn't bring myself to break up with Dina. On April 4th, 1980, after only knowing each other a little more than two months, we got married. I was feeling guilty about not following the Lord, and caving in to my own stupid weaknesses, but God did some amazing things that day to show his blessings on our marriage.

On the way to get married, we were picking up our witnesses, John and Hessy. As I was backing out of John's driveway, I accidentally drove off the edge of the bridge that went over a big drainage culvert. We all looked at each other without saying a word in wonderment of what we should do. Our back wheel was hanging in midair and I was scared to even get out of the car to look for fear that the whole car might go off the edge. Before we could even begin to talk among ourselves, from out of nowhere, up drives a garbage truck with four men on it. Without saying a word, they each lifted a corner of the car, set it back on the driveway and drove away. We all looked at each other in amazement. To this day I believe that they were angels.

Then as we met Reverend Morrison at the church he shared with me that during his preparation for our marriage ceremony, he had sensed the presence of God like never before. I think his words were,

"I have married hundreds of couples, but I've never felt God's blessing on any of them like I have on this one" Although I never stopped regretting choosing to get married over accepting God's calling, I carried the events of the angels and his blessing on the ceremony as God's approval of our wedding. I don't know how many times during our rocky twenty-eight years of marriage that in a difficult time, I recalled those events and rather than giving up, I continued in our marriage.

Chapter Fifteen
Saved and Married but Never Quite on Course

Was I an idiot or what? I was passing up an amazing opportunity to serve God and getting married to someone who had as many bad marriages as I had. And I was doing it without even really knowing her. It didn't seem quite so stupid at the time, but as I said, I still felt I had made a wrong move. But God doesn't waste opportunities. Dina said she was a Christian woman who was drawn to my spirituality, and she needed someone to help her raise her boys, so we moved on. But as we moved on we disagreed on just about everything. She was a Sunday school teacher for young married couples at her Baptist church, and I continued at True Light. She thought I should quit and join her at her church, and I felt called to stay at True Light. Finally, her pastor told her that she should follow me so we all went to True Light.

She was supportive of my decision to work the paper route and volunteer with *The Old Time Religion Hour*, where I was continuing to grow spiritually. I was beginning to hear the Holy Spirit's voice so clearly. For example, when I was delivering papers through the apartments, I would hear God regularly say, "Take an extra paper with you." Every time that happened, sure enough, I would end up throwing a paper on the roof or on a wrong porch. I would normally carry fifteen to twenty papers through each apartment complex based on customer count and with God's help, I always had the right amount of papers even when I had made a mistake.

While promoting the proposed Christian Television Station for *The Old Time Religion Hour*, I crossed paths with a few interesting and sometimes famous Christian personalities. One of those was Wally Wood. He had devoted his life to the study of biblical end-times and comparing current events to those prophesied in the Bible.

I went to one of his presentations and was amazed. His predictions of the events leading up to and during the reign of the Antichrist were almost the same as many of the plans and events I had seen in my visions several years earlier. Wally and I became friends and we regularly discussed his interpretations of scripture concerning the end-times.

Although Dina said she was attracted to me because of my spirituality, almost from the time we got married, Dina tried to change everything about me. She told me she had been a Christian ever since she was seven and it just wasn't correct to spend three hours a day in the Bible. She said that the church would teach us everything we need to know. I couldn't question that fact that she had been in the church a lot longer than me, but I just couldn't tear myself away from the scriptures. We also disagreed about how the boys should be raised. Mark was a naturally good boy who was very organized and meticulous, but Robert was a mess. I don't think his room had ever been cleaned or his bed made. To walk into his room, you had to clear a path on the floor in the six to eight-inch deep layer of toys and trash. He was intelligent but was a terrible student. He had no structure or discipline in his life.

And neither of the boys knew how to act in public. Dina believed if she disciplined the boys their spirits would be broken. She clearly didn't understand how to discipline with love. I put all of myself into raising the boys, but because Dina ridiculed almost everything I did, I had only limited success.

There were a few things that I would not give in on though. One was Robert's education. He was about to fail first or second grade, I don't remember which, and the school wanted to hold him back, and I knew that was the right thing to do. Dina said the only way she would let that happen was if they could convince Robert it was his idea. They succeeded, and he repeated the grade.

It was extremely frustrating to have Dina constantly interfering with me trying to get the boys on the right track. I apparently made progress though, because several of the leaders of Dina's church told me that they could see a remarkable improvement in both boys. I tried to get the boys on a more balanced diet as well. As we established better-eating habits, Mark used to joke about the meals they used to eat before I entered the picture.

After about a year of our marriage, I was offered an opportunity to be a steel detailer trainee at a steel fabrication shop for ten dollars an hour. Things were thin living on Dina's paycheck and my paper route, so I took it and quit my paper route and left *The Old Time Religion Hour* as well. I had mixed feelings about leaving that ministry because God had used that situation to teach me so much. But after a considerable amount of prayer, I felt God wanted me to move on. The new job quickly became a very interesting situation and a tremendous opportunity for spiritual growth. Although the position that was offered was a training position to learn how to draw steel members for buildings, there was no trainer, my orientation was, "Here are the blueprints for the project we're doing. There are the blueprints and the shop drawings for a similar project we just completed. You'll probably be able to compare them and figure it out. Oh, and by the way, the men are downstairs in the shop waiting for your shop drawings."

Talk about an impossible task, I had never seen an actual set of blueprints before and had only seen shop drawings from my time at the oilfield equipment company. They were similar but only vaguely. I had no textbook to use to learn the tolerances for drawing, I had to learn everything by comparing the previous project drawings. What made it worse, was that, in the previous project, all the buildings were square with each other, but in the new project, all the buildings were joined at an angle to each other. I needed some serious trigonometry to figure out the connections, something I hadn't used in probably fifteen years.

I went to a technical bookstore and bought a shop math book and figured it out. To this day I don't know how I got through that first project. I prayed a lot and I remember several nights sitting in the office drawing in tears until near midnight. I also had to draw the stair pieces. I now know in hindsight that before the invention of AutoCAD, even experienced steel detailers struggled with stair drawings. Somehow, I think primarily by God's intervention, the pieces were pretty much correct. I later had to go to Corpus Christi to the job site to show how the pieces fit together. That taught me even more than I learned drawing them, and because now I had been through the whole fabrication and erection process, I was better prepared for the next project.

The company was very small and gave me opportunities to grow into whatever position I might choose. Within a few months, I started estimating costs for new projects. Cecil, the owner of the company was sharp, but didn't seem to have a lot of experience at estimating. And there wasn't anyone else there to give me any serious insight into how to do any of the new things I was learning. Every time I started training for a new position, it was up to me to figure out how to do it. But I did a lot of praying and God seemed to direct me to excel in every area.

While I was growing spiritually through my challenges at work and ministry challenges at True Light, my marriage with Dina was struggling. The leadership at True Light convinced me that I had been called to preach, so they licensed me to preach and eventually ordained me as a Missionary Baptist Minister. God's hand seemed to be on my career and ministry, but at home, we couldn't get together on anything. I felt like I was doing all the right things biblically, but Dina and I seemed to be reading different Bibles.

A major turning point in our marriage took place one Saturday when I took Mark to his Saturday bowling league. When I returned home, I confided in Dina that I had felt aroused by some of the young teenage girls at the bowling alley. I confided and confessed in hope that she would pray with me on that issue, but instead, she went crazy. Although I had come from a very promiscuous lifestyle, I hadn't had a problem with lust or attractions for other women since I'd become a Christian and I was concerned. I don't remember all the names she called me and all the accusations she made, but I do remember that our marriage was totally different after that day.

Between our disagreements about raising the boys and now this new problem, things began to get unbearable. About a year and a half into the marriage, I decided, I just couldn't take it anymore and decided to get a divorce. Just before I told Dina my decision, she told me she was pregnant. I decided at that moment that I was not going to let another child of mine grow up without a father, and somehow, no matter what it took, I would not get a divorce.

God's hand continued to be on me at work, as I gained the ability to pray my way through estimating and bidding new work. Each time I would submit a bid for new work, I was consistently just a few dollars lower than the other bidders. It happened so often that my competitors accused me of having inside information, When I told people that I was praying through my bids, they didn't believe me. Because of God's hand on me, both I and my company were becoming a center of attention. We were getting bigger and bigger projects and I was starting to get offers from other companies.

In August of 1982, our daughter Stacie was born. It was an amazing time for a lot of reasons. At the fabrication shop, I was working two shifts because I had decided that I wanted to be a part of the entire fabrication process of a project we were doing at the time. It was the largest project we'd been awarded since I'd been there. It was a four-story building that required approximately four hundred tons of steel. I thought that if I laid out and cut every piece of material in the project, I would have a better understanding of the fabrication process and make me a better estimator. Besides working a double shift, we were redecorating Stacie's room. I was only getting a few hours of sleep a night during that time, but the incredible experience of the birth of my Stacie was more than enough to keep me going.

After we completed the four-story project, I continued to get offers to work for other companies. For a long time, I didn't pay any attention to the offers. But as Cecil's company made more and more money, I felt like he was not spending the money wisely. It was his company, but customers were starting to look at me as the steam behind the company's success and I wanted to see us use the profits to build a solid company that would take care of us all.

After several months of disagreeing with Cecil, I decided to accept an offer and move to a big steel erection company. They offered me quite a bit more money and lots of opportunities. They had worked all over Houston and Dallas and their projects were considerably larger than Cecil's. Some of their projects were as many as twenty stories and almost all of them were more than ten stories. The best thing about it was that as an erector, I got to work with fabricators that were a lot bigger than Cecil's company. As we erected their fabricated steel, I had the opportunity to visit their shops and see how the larger companies operated.

I loved my new job and was taking advantage of every opportunity to learn from these bigger players in the steel construction business. I worked primarily as an estimator, but because of my background in fabrication and producing shop drawings, I was called on regularly to go to our job sites and evaluate problems.

After I was with the erection company for a little over a year, for the first time in my life, I got to take a one-week vacation with pay. But shortly after returning from vacation, the company started having problems with the IRS and the employees started to scatter. I had remained friends with Cecil and he invited me to come back to work for him.

Cecil didn't have much work at the time, while I was pretty much on a roll. I had met some new potential customers while I was with the erection company and I was very interested in rejoining Cecil, if he would let me run the company, including the financial decisions. He agreed, and we were underway. I decided that before we started working on revamping the finances, we needed to get a backlog of projects on the books. So, I went out and got us some contracts. Things were slowing down in Houston at that time because the oil boom was over, but I was still able to land some nice projects. Once we started mobilizing to start the work, I began to look at the finances of the company and found that the company was in serious debt. So much debt that we wouldn't have the ability to complete the contracts that I'd just landed. It was obvious that we either needed some outside financing help or needed to start a new company. So I began looking for an investor.

As I said, things had slowed down in Houston, but the fact that I had a few good projects, spoke well for my abilities. I found two men that were both willing to back me in business, but both refused to allow Cecil into the deal. I wanted to remain loyal to Cecil because despite our disagreements, we were friends and I appreciated the opportunities he had given me. Both investors were adamant that they would not back me if Cecil was going to be included. I considered Cecil a friend and didn't want to abandon him, so I continued to look for other potential investors.

Several weeks later, I was contacted by the owner of an oil field derrick fabrication company that had a very impressive facility, a fat bank account, and no work. He offered me forty percent of a new company that we would form as well as the position of running the company as president. But he too saw Cecil as a liability rather than an asset. The contracts that I had recently landed, needed to be fabricated and I was running out of time. So, although I didn't want to cut Cecil out of the deal, I felt I had no choice. I agreed, and I was now a partner in what was to be a major fabrication company. I got a company car and an expense account, which was very nice, but best of all, I now had all the resources I needed to compete for almost any project. We had a huge facility, state of the art equipment and strong financial backing. We even had a fax machine, something I'd never heard of.

I hired several of the best estimators in town, and we were off and running. God's hand remained on me as well. In a slow Houston construction market, we started filling the shop with work. We got so busy we had to add a second shift. Our shop was in extreme northwest Houston I lived in southwest Houston and True Light was in extreme northeast Houston. To drive the triangle was nearly 100 miles. Dina and I had come to a point where we felt at peace about leaving True Light and started looking for a church closer to our home. We found a Bible Church in Alief, Texas and moved our membership.

As I reflect on True Light and the role it played in my story, I'd like to share a few milestone events that I will carry with me for the rest of my life. First, one morning when I was entering the sanctuary of True Light, I felt a rush of energy hit me as I opened the door. It was like a gust of wind, but it was coming from the inside of the church. As I pondered what had happened, I sensed the Holy Spirit tell me that what I had felt, was the power of the love of the people in the church for one another. It was such a memorable experience, that I remember it to this day, I still pray every day that the power of love that I felt that day would be present in my house today to the extent that everyone who comes to my door and everyone who walks by my house would feel it.

The second thing that I consider noteworthy, is an experience I had in one of our prayer meetings. You may remember that I had lots of bad experiences growing up in Hempstead that caused me to have some bad feelings towards black people. My time with the True Light church family had erased a lot of those feelings. I had developed relationships with Reverend Morrison, his family and some of the other families in the church that were filled with love, but some of the childhood memories persisted. One night as we were holding hands and praying at True Light, the Holy Spirit spoke to me and asked the question, "can you tell the color of the person you are holding hands with?" I obviously couldn't, but that experience triggered a change in the way I instinctively look at people. The world blames racism for a lot of things, but the truth is, we instinctively separate ourselves from others because of our differences. Different color, different gender, different appearance, different culture, different political views and a multitude of other differences divide us.

Some months later, I had a conversation with a black friend when he shared an experience he had at an all-white party. He was well-educated, always well-groomed and had impeccable manners. He shared that everyone at the party was so nice to him and he felt like he was one of them. He went on to speculate that if he wore braided hair, he was sure that they would have acted differently towards him. I spoke up and said, if I had worn braided hair and showed up at the party, they would have acted differently towards me. He was thoughtfully silent for a minute, then agreed. Admit it or not, everyone including myself is intolerant of others who think, look or behave differently than we do.

I learned a lot of things about relationships at True Light. I developed relationships with church members and members of the community that I met through the church that I still cherish today as some of the best relationships of my life.

There's one last thing that I observed at True Light that I still regularly ponder. It is the power of the Gospel message. I've commented that I felt the theology taught by Reverend Morrison was not very deep. To me, it seemed to be all milk and no meat. But there was an undeniable power in every message he delivered. He would end every message with a word picture of how Jesus was crucified, buried and resurrected in payment for our sins. He spoke of the gospel, and the Holy Spirit seemed to overcome him as he spoke. He didn't use emotion provoking music while he spoke as we sometimes see in the movies, but there was no denying that the power of the Holy Spirit would sweep through the church and there would almost always be people in the pews that would be overcome by the spirit.

There were times, I experienced being overcome by the Holy Spirit as well. I point this out because we live in a time when many preachers feel like they need to be relevant to their listeners, so they sparingly mention the gospel in their sermons. I admit to being one of those who rarely includes the gospel in my messages. And I've begun to question the wisdom in that.

Allow me to use one more illustration. The late Dr. Billy Graham spoke in a similar fashion. His message was never that complicated, nor was he ever overcome by the Holy Spirit that I know of, yet he always clearly preached the simple gospel in his messages and he won hundreds of thousands or maybe millions for Christ. There is a power in the gospel that I still don't understand, and I feel that we are overlooking it today. I'm thankful for my experience at True Light that continues to live within me. I feel blessed to have been a part of that body of believers for the season God gave me there.

Early on in our time at the new church in Alief, Dina started a campaign with the pastor to get me to spend less time with God and more time with her. I was still naïve to some things in the faith and she convinced him that I was neglecting her to spend time with God. He suggested that I should put my time with my wife higher on my priority list than my time with God. Today, now that I know better, I recognize that advice as unbiblical. I agree that my wife and my family should be my first ministry priority, but I don't believe I can carry out that ministry effectively unless my relationship with God is intact and healthy.

I had reached a point of spiritual growth that convinced me that my daily time with God is what gave me the strength to respond correctly to life's issues and daily challenges. But the pastor was my authority figure, so in submission, I went along with his suggestion, but as I look back, it was that change in my priorities that caused my life to take a turn onto the road of becoming religious rather than being a committed Christian. Simply stated, my fire for God was gradually all but put out.

My new work and church schedules gave me lots of time with Stacie. She was at the age where we would go for walks every evening after supper and look at the flowers in the yards of our neighbors. She would regularly run over to the flowers, smell them and say, "Mells Good!" Those walks with Stacie are some my best memories as a father. During that same time, we also moved Robert into a private school to see if we could improve his grades. He was still seriously struggling.

His teacher in the private school was one of the owners and she had Robert's number from day one. She realized he was seriously under-achieving and she didn't let him get away with anything. Dina hated her because Robert complained about her teaching methods constantly. As a result, Dina and I argued about it most of the time. Finally, after only one year and against my better judgment, I agreed to let him go back to public school. After Robert finished that year in the private school, he tested out three grades higher than when he had entered. I feel that that school was probably the best thing that ever happened to him as far as his education.

Meanwhile, due to the success of our fabrication company, I was contacted by a General Contractor who had received the Construction Management contract for Houston's new convention center. They invited me to meet with them and I was flattered. When we met, they told me that they were impressed with our company's growth and wanted to know if I would like to help them price the steel portion of the new convention center project.

Again, I was flattered and accepted. The deal was that I would have thirty days to estimate the steel fabrication and erection portion of the project at no charge to the city, but our company would be recognized in the bid documents as the company that did the steel budget. At the time I agreed, I had not seen the bid documents. As I was leaving it took six of us to carry the documents to the car. There had to be five hundred pounds of blueprints and specifications. I was more than overwhelmed. I'd never seen plans that large, but I was too embarrassed to say anything. I thanked them for the opportunity and took the plans home.

When I go home, I took the plans out of the car and put them on my dining room table without unrolling them. For a week they lay there untouched while I tried to figure out what to do. I was too embarrassed to give them back, but was totally overwhelmed by the sight and the size of the plans. After I don't know how many times of passing the documents on my table and after a lot of prayer, I finally decided to unroll the plans and looked at them. I discovered that the plans were not that complicated, the project was just massive. As I looked at the plans, it occurred to me that if I were to break the steel into five categories of fabrication I could subcontract the portions out to other major fabricators that specialized in those categories.

There were huge pipe columns made of rolled plate. There were hundreds of steel trusses. There was a standard structural steel, joist, and decking package. There was a miscellaneous metals package. And finally, there was an ornamental metals package. I spent the next few days looking for the best plate roller and the best truss manufacturer available. I decided that I would do the structural steel package at our shop and I knew qualified people in the other two categories. I met with all of them and told them we would live and die as a team. They all agreed, and we went to work. We ended up hitting the actual budget within less than one percent.

We didn't get the contract, but this episode made me an international player in the construction industry. Our name and projected budget numbers for that project went out to many of the major players in the construction industry all over the United States. We started getting invitations to bid work all over the world.

But as our company grew, my partner began to change. He went out of his way to degrade me in front of the employees and seemed to have an agenda to squeeze me out. I tried to not let it bother me, but it was creating knots in my stomach. He had controlling interest in the company and could do pretty much anything he wanted to. One day he called me into his office and told me he was taking over as president of the company. It bothered me, but because I knew that most of the employees could see what was happening, I didn't put up a fight and continued business as usual. But while I didn't let on that I'd had enough, I started praying and asking God what my next move should be.

I prayed from April until October, putting out fleece after fleece to be sure I was hearing God correctly. The company had grown to where my share of the company was worth a significant amount, probably more than a million dollars. But now I began to feel that God was directing me to leave the company and go out on my own. He had shown me so many times and in so many ways that I should leave until there was no doubt in my mind that I should go. At the beginning of October, after a considerable period of prayer concerning my exit strategy, I began moving the things from my office each night in my briefcase.

I also began to gradually delegate my projects to other people on my staff. By the last day of October 1986, everything was gone from my office except the paintings on the wall and every project had been delegated to someone else. Nobody in the company had a clue that I was leaving. I bought a new car that night because I'd been driving a company car, and I was ready to make my exit.

On November first, I had Dina follow me to work in her car and I got to the office early. I put the paintings from my office in her car and when my partner arrived, I presented him with a simple written agreement with a unique provision, that I would sign my entire ownership in the company over to him if I never had to see or talk to him again. He signed it immediately, I gave him the keys to the company car and walked out the door.

Chapter Sixteen
Self-employed with No Partners

I felt total relief when I walked out the door, but it didn't take long for the reality of the moment to set in. I didn't have much debt, but I didn't have much in the bank either. I had quite a few customers who had become friends, but I really hadn't said much to anyone about leaving for fear of giving my secret away. I didn't have a fabrication shop either. There was my friend Gary, who had told me he had a small shop at his house if I ever needed any fabrication done. So, I called him the day I left to make sure that the shop was still available. When I found out it was, I started peddling steel. I was able to get a few small projects right away, but nothing of any size.

By December tenth, I was out of work, out of money and seriously second guessing my decision to part ways with my previous partner. Dina and I hadn't done any Christmas shopping and needed groceries. The only thing I knew to do is pray. And what a prayer it was. I got down on my knees in my office in my house and in tears, asked God what He had done to me. I repeated to him the entire process that I'd gone through until I was sure I was doing the right thing, and here I was with no work and no money.

As I was finishing the prayer, the phone rang. It was one of my customers with an emergency. They had just completed a high rise building with a six-story parking garage and they had built the perimeter walls of the garage six inches too short. They needed a six-inch rail around every floor of the garage immediately and asked me if I could do it. I told him yes but didn't have the money to do the project without an advance. He told me to be at his office in thirty minutes and they'd have a check for me. I took the job and by subcontracting it out, we got it completed by Christmas Eve and we had one of the best Christmases we'd ever had.

By the end of January, I had a good backlog of work and twenty thousand dollars in the bank. What a God we have! For the next several years my new company went on to grow into a successful steel fabrication/erection company that specialized in difficult projects. Within a year I had offices in Houston, Springfield, Virginia and the Boston area. Construction was booming in the Northeast and slow in Houston, so I was getting contracts in the northeast for premium dollars and subcontracting the work at competitive prices to Houston fabricators who needed work. We were doing extremely well until one of my customers burned me for $145,000. They were a big company that lost money on the project, (not because of me), so they found a questionable legal loophole and didn't pay me.

That almost buried me, but somehow, we survived, by God's provision. By the beginning of 1989, I was having serious problems at home with Dina and Robert and I was beginning to get a little discouraged with the steel business. Between new OSHA regulations and changes in workers compensation and general liability insurance guidelines, it was getting more and more difficult to do business. I think it could also have been that things at home were finally beginning to affect my attitude in everything I did. Robert was now approaching driving age and Dina wanted me to give him driving privileges with no strings attached. He was barely getting through school and was not responsible for anything he did other than high school football. I saw the privilege of driving to be our last opportunity to get Robert on the right track before adulthood.

I had a notion about going to Eastern Europe, which was in the process of opening to western business. I wanted to go teach business classes to entrepreneurs. I had become politically active and knew my congressman well enough to get an appointment to see what he thought about the idea and the possibilities of getting a government grant to fund the class. We met, and he tried to discourage me about Eastern Europe, but encouraged me to check out West Africa. He gave me a contact who I met with and in March of 1989, I made my first trip to West Africa. I was there primarily for business, but during that week we did a lot of sightseeing.

Africa is an amazing place. We visited two of the slave trading castles in Cape Coast and Elmina. That is something that every American should experience. What we've been taught in the US, is that the slaves and black culture were exploited solely by whites, but that's not the case at all. While it's true that the whites of British and Dutch origin were the ones that bought, transported and sold the slaves, I didn't realize that the slaves were captured, warehoused and delivered to the traders by the elite African tribes. Their own people. I was so moved by the visit to the castles, I made a point of taking everyone who later visited me in Africa, to see what I'd seen. The slave trade business was so inhumane, that everyone that I took on the tours of the castles was deeply touched.

The man that took me on that first trip seemed to know everyone in business and the government. During the time I spent investigating business opportunities there, I felt like a kid in a candy store. There was also a more personal side of me that was more like an animal let out of its cage. I had been miserable during the previous nine years of marriage, but for some reason, I finally felt free. Until now I'd been a faithful husband, but again, for some reason, I suddenly felt the freedom to do whatever I felt like doing. I was there for business, but with opportunities for infidelity presenting themselves constantly, and I eventually gave in.

During that week I was there on my first trip, I attended an entrepreneurs' workshop where I met several men that had businesses with great products but no money to promote their business ideas. And the money they were looking for was not much by American standards. I immediately thought that if I was to set up a business incubator that paired up American entrepreneurs with African entrepreneurs I could help a lot of businesses get started which would help both countries. I had considerable experience as an American entrepreneur with limited financing. I had been successful in the steel business but found it extremely difficult to build up enough financial momentum to perform major projects. But the limited funds that I did have access to were considerably more than what these African businessmen needed to launch their businesses.

I thought that if I could match American entrepreneurs with their technology and a small amount of funding with the African entrepreneurs that had learned to operate on a shoestring and had established markets, the partnerships would be profitable for both sides and both countries. Everyone with whom I shared the idea, loved it. I made several more trips back to Africa to investigate further and by July of 1989, I was ready to make a presentation to that West African country's government for their approval. For the big presentation, I took one of my Houston customers with me to evaluate my presentation to the government and to help gauge the governments' reception to my proposal.

As we were exiting the meeting, I asked my friend what he thought about my presentation. His reply was that he wanted to open a construction company there and he wanted me to run it. That reply told me that my presentation must have been pretty good, I was encouraged, but I really wasn't ready to settle in with only one client. But I was running low on money, I was totally infatuated with doing business in West Africa and I was desperate for a way to stay married without having to live in the same house with Dina and Robert. At that time I was making a six-figure annual income in the steel business. My friend offered me a partial ownership in the new construction company, but the salary would be only half of what I was making in the US, but in addition, there would be a generous expense allowance to run the company. He also promised that as soon as the African company was making money, I would be raised to at least what I was making in the states, so I accepted the offer.

It was my hope that Dina and Stacie would move to Africa with me, but she maintained that she didn't have anyone to leave Robert with. So, in October of 1989, I closed my steel business, packed up and moved to West Africa by myself.

Chapter Seventeen
Off to Conquer Africa

As I formulated my plans to get started, I found that the laws in that country stated that every business had to have at least a ten percent ownership by a native of their country, so the first issue was to find a qualified local partner. I thought that the best path to that goal was to interview people that already were in the construction business and see what they'd done on their own. I interviewed several business owners and narrowed it down to two. One was in general construction with most of their work being in road construction. The other was also in general construction but primarily a home builder. I decided to first check out the road construction company which took me on a forty-eight-hour journey that covered the length and width of the country, an area like the size of Oregon.

When I asked to see their equipment, I didn't know it was parked all over the country. Their custom was that when they completed a road project, they parked their equipment near that project until they found out where the next contract would be located. Our travels took us to the extreme west, north, east and south boundaries of their country. We had to use a jungle ferry across a river, we traveled roads that were overgrown with four-foot deep foliage and went to areas where people had never seen white people before. It was an exciting but sometimes scary adventure.

After that, I checked out the home builder, my first reaction was to try and partner with both companies. But it didn't take any time at all for me to realize that neither of them would agree to that. So, I ended up choosing the home builder. The homes that he had completed looked good. The construction all seemed plumb and level and his corners were crisp. Everything I looked at appeared to be done accurately and professionally. And he and his wife were both professing Christians. I arranged a meeting with both the

American partner and my newly chosen African partners and we completed all necessary agreements. I was appointed Managing Director and by May of 1990, we had received our first commercial contract. We began building houses as well.

As chance, (or God's plan), would have it, as we were starting our new company the World Bank was introducing a new mortgage program for that country. Until that time all the houses being built in the country had been built on a cash basis and they always took more than a year to build. If the country was going to have a mortgage program they were going to have to find someone that could build houses at a lot faster pace and in a lot larger volume than anyone in the country was currently doing. I told the managers of the mortgage program that we could build houses in approximately eight weeks and at a rate of approximately four hundred units per year which met the requirements of the mortgage program.

I don't think anyone believed it, but they had no other options. No other builder in the country was able to make a construction proposal that remotely compared to ours and if the program managers couldn't convince the World Bank that they could produce a substantial number of houses annually, they would lose the mortgage program money. They asked for proof, and I completed and showed them a business plan that projected the cash flow from time of startup to point of producing at a rate of four hundred houses per year.

The next thing we had to do was prove that we could build a house in eight weeks. We finished our first four-plex unit in five weeks. We not only finished the four-plex early, but I made a deal with several of the local furniture manufacturers to furnish the units as models. No one in the country had ever displayed fully furnished model homes before. We scheduled a grand opening press conference, I arranged to have both the American Ambassador and that country's Secretary of Works and Housing speak. It was an amazing success with extensive television coverage and our company was off to a grand start.

As I said earlier, my natural abilities are promotion and idea development. Now that I'd used my promoting abilities, it was time to kick the idea development abilities into gear. It's one thing to build four houses in five weeks, but it's something totally different to start building houses at a rate of four hundred units per year. How was I going to organize a workforce that was accustomed to building houses on a one- year schedule into a group that can do it in eight weeks? And the bigger task than that was how would we be able to duplicate those teams into a workforce that can be working on as many as sixty-four homes that were to be under construction at the same time?

An idea came to me while I was back in Houston for a visit. I was standing in line at MacDonald's and it hit me as I watched the employees work. I thought that senior management has broken down the operation of the restaurant into a series of jobs. And once an employee had been trained in any one or more of those jobs, they could work effectively in any of the company's restaurants around the world. I thought, why couldn't I similarly break down the process of building a house into a series of jobs that would apply to the construction of any of our houses?

When I returned to Africa, I designed the list of jobs for each trade and a construction schedule that would be posted in front of each house. The schedule listed what jobs had to be completed each day by each trade for the house to be completed in eight weeks. I also designed a reward and penalty system for the trade supervisors to ensure that everyone completed the jobs on time and as they were designed to be done. It took a little while to get the system in full motion because these concepts were totally foreign to everyone including my African partner.

I remember the battle to accept this process, with one of the masonry supervisors. He was very talented but insisted that he was going to do things his way. We fired and rehired him three times before he finally decided we were serious. The last time we rehired him, we made him wait thirty days before we put him back on the schedule. Every morning at seven o'clock he would stand in line for employment but was not selected. From that point on, he was our best mason. It took a while, but once all the trade supervisors realized we were serious about our system, they all fell in line and we were building houses at the rate we had projected.

The next obstacle we faced was that property title transfer had always been a one-year process as well. What is our motivation to build houses in eight-weeks if we couldn't get paid until title had been transferred in a year? I raised the question, and they didn't have an answer. So I asked permission to let us walk a title transfer request through their system to understand the process and see how the system could be streamlined. Again, they had no other options and agreed. We found that more than ninety percent of the time was consumed by requests sitting in department in-boxes. We asked if they could reassign a few of their people for us to train in rapid title transfer and again they agreed. By the time we finished the training, titles were being transferred in thirty days or less. From that point on we began to gain momentum and my projections quickly began being met on schedule.

But just because we had the locals trained and on track, didn't mean I was without problems. The biggest challenge I had there was getting our management people to go along with me when I wanted to try new ideas. My ideas were new to them, but they were things we'd been doing in construction successfully for years in the States. And before I could approach our senior supervisors, I first had to convince my African partner. I don't know how many times he would say, "That will never work". When I would finally convince him to trust me and the idea worked, he would always say, "I can't believe it worked". I'm not trying to paint myself as a genius here because as I said, I never asked them to try anything that wasn't a basic and proven concept in the U.S.

I also had an American partner who regularly hounded me about finances. My business plan clearly showed that we would have several months of negative cash flow before it turned positive and as things progressed, everything we were doing showed us to be following the plan exactly. Even our banker said that he'd never seen such an accurate business plan. Despite that, each week when we drew down our scheduled amount from our bank line of credit, my American partner would call and tell me that he wasn't going to put any more money into the company. Each time I had to go through the same speech and reassure him that everything was on schedule.

Once we reached the point of positive cash flow (on schedule), my job began to change from organizing our workforce to expediting our suppliers. We couldn't get cement blocks or wooden doors fast enough, so we set up a block manufacturing operation at our sub-division and decided for large acquisitions of doors and windows. Next came the challenge of acquiring land for building sub-divisions. The tribal chiefs controlled all the land in the country and the methods of acquiring land from them were pretty much established, but our needs required some new thinking. Land prices were reasonable, but every deal was a cash deal and people had rarely purchased tracts of land the size we were looking for.

Most of our money was still tied up in the expansion of the construction so we didn't have the kind of cash necessary to purchase land the standard way. I formulated a purchase plan agreement for the chiefs where rather than get paid everything up front at a low price, we would make a sizable down payment and pay them a better unit price as we sold each parcel of property with a house on it. Understand that in many third world countries, people assume you're dishonest until you prove yourself otherwise, so this was not an easy plan to explain let alone sell. But after taking several runs at selling the idea, I finally found a chief that understood the benefits of what we were offering and sold us I think it was twenty-seven acres. After that, my job became a lot easier and we started selling houses like crazy. Before long we had a ninety-day waiting period for starts on new sales. Nearly every decision I made, turned out to be correct and every new idea was successful. I almost felt like I could do nothing wrong.

As the company grew, I became a celebrity. I was on television regularly and on the guest list of all the embassy parties as well as most of the country's VIP parties. My African partner was catching on quickly and after about six months of success, my work became more social and public relations than management. I was always networking and making new contacts as well as creating new options for our business growth. We were looking at expanding to other areas of the country and I was thoroughly enjoying it.

We were so successful that I was beginning to raise concerns with the government. I didn't know it for a while, but the president of the country had me constantly under surveillance. I had gotten to be pretty good friends with several of the president's cabinet secretaries. One night I was at one of their houses for dinner. He had several bottles of wine and started laughing about the government concerns about my plans for the country. He knew me well enough to know that I was just doing what I was hired to do as Managing Director of the construction company, but on a continent where government takeovers are a regular event, none of the seated presidents like to see anyone get too popular. He told me I was almost always one of the first topics to come up at the weekly cabinet meetings. He said the president would always ask, "What's that Passler been up to this week." I asked my friend, the secretary, why he just didn't speak up and tell them what he knew about me? He said he was having too much fun listening to the reports and interpretations concerning my activities.

That was my life in West Africa. As our success grew, so did my pride and ego. I still went to church on Sundays and most of my close friends were missionaries. I tried to share the financial benefits of my expense allowance with them by buying dinners and just sharing in general, but although we were close I could tell that a lot of things in my lifestyle made them uncomfortable. But I really needed them as my Christian lifeline. I was doing some things that I knew were wrong, primarily my casual adulterous relationships. I had drifted from some of the other Christian standards that I had maintained in the states, but I felt like as long as I kept close ties with my missionary friends, I wouldn't drift too far. I met for a weekly accountability breakfast with four mission group leaders, so I knew that they would be asking me questions. I carried that with me all week and the thought of that meeting loomed over my every social action. In hindsight, I had become a spiritual mess and my moral compass was totally out of whack, but for some reason at the time, I felt I was still doing okay. Who knows how far I would have strayed if it weren't for that group of men?

I'd gone from being a strong, committed Christian during my first few years of conversion, to a lukewarm churchgoer during the years prior to going to Africa. From there I'd become someone who was really starting to question my faith.

I had some secular friends as well while I was there. Stuart and Doreen have transplanted Brits who had lived in West Africa for years. They had a place at the beach where they spent the weekends. They were great hosts and I could always count on finding a group of interesting and friendly people there when I visited. And they always had a Sunday afternoon feast. I really miss my time with them. On Saturdays, I played softball with the folks from the American embassy. I loved playing softball and baseball. (Several people told me when I was growing up that I should have tried to play professional baseball. That was a dream that I let get by.) I had several friends that worked at the embassy, and spending time with them helped to make life very good there. The only thing I missed was my daughter Stacie. I made over a dozen trips home during that first year and a half, but it wasn't the same, just seeing her for a week at a time.

As my head and my popularity grew, I had to navigate through a multitude of opportunities and temptations, and I didn't do well with a lot of my decisions. I was not only a celebrity among the locals but with the international community as well. I chose to bask in the glory of my success and indulge in almost every opportunity that came my way because of that fame. In simple terms, I was living a life that was very self-serving and my Christian life was becoming less and less of a priority.

Then came one specific event that was to become a turning point in my life there in West Africa. I was invited to a dinner at the home of the director of one of the major British companies there. During dinner, I sat across from a visiting World Bank executive and he made the statement that many of his colleagues within his own organization as well as some with the United Nations considered me to be one of the most impactful individuals ever to come to West Africa. As everyone at the table listened, He went on to list a few of my notable accomplishments and asked how I was able to be so effective in my dealings there. I remember that as I opened my mouth to answer, I sensed the Holy Spirit inside me telling me this was an opportunity to glorify God. I don't really remember what my response was, but it wasn't glorifying to God, I claimed the glory for myself.

It was only a few days later when I was out walking alone on one of our sub-divisions, that I heard a voice so clear that I turned around to see where it was coming from. I saw no one, but the voice told me, that I was not being a very good steward of the blessings God had showered on me and He was going to take me down.

We were only a few weeks from having our first annual stockholders meeting to review the progress and profits of our first year. I knew we had made a lot of money, I think it was something like 1.7 million dollars profit. I was anticipating a sizable pay raise as I had been promised and to receive praise from my partners for a job well done. Instead, the first order of business was to give the African partner a raise and rather than giving me a raise, they voted to deduct my living expenses from my annual profit sharing check.

I was furious. I resigned on the spot and told them that within thirty days, I would be gone. I agreed to train my replacement and sell my ownership stake back to them for far less than it was worth, I didn't think through any of those actions, it was my emotions and my big head doing the talking, and once again, I found myself on my own.

When the word got out that I was leaving the construction company, I was flooded with offers. I spent a month or so just listening to them all. The most interesting offer came from the World Bank. They had a team there auditing all the businesses that they had helped fund. There were approximately 1,200 companies that were either broke or on the verge of being broke. Almost all of them had assets with a value of at least a million dollars, but they had run out of funding. They gave me a profile of each of those businesses and told me that if I felt I could turn any of them into a profitable business, I could have the business if I would pay off its loans from the World Bank.

As I began to review the profiles, I was amazed at the assets and potential of all these struggling or totally abandoned businesses. Once again, I felt like a kid in a candy store. There were companies that had never even opened, some had thousands of dollars' worth of equipment still in crates that had never been opened. Honestly, many of them were so vast that I couldn't even get my mind around how to revive them. I looked seriously at a few, but always had a hard time trying to work out a deal with the person with the 10% local ownership.

During those negotiations, I began to better understand businesses and what makes them successful. To me running a business was second nature, but I saw that all the local owners had degrees that qualified them academically to manage the business, but very few if any of the businesses had an entrepreneur at the helm to be the driving force that gives a business sustained life. I assume these owners had the mentality of an employee and not the heart to give the business life. Nor did they understand the mentality of being committed to making a situation work. Their mentality was to do the best job they could as long as there was funding, but after that, they were no longer committed to the business. I hope World Bank has learned what was obvious to me, it takes more than a leader with degrees behind his name to make a business successful, it takes an entrepreneur.

After several months of negotiations, I reached a point of realizing that it was time to go back to Houston. I had left the African construction company in May of 1992 and promised Dina that if I hadn't made a deal on a new venture by Labor Day, I would come back home. So, Labor Day of 1992, I headed back to Houston.

Chapter Eighteen
Starting Over in Houston

It's a long plane ride back to Houston, nearly twenty hours, so there was plenty of time to think. I had a pretty good attitude because although I hadn't been able to strike a deal on a new business, all that happened in the last several months there concerning business had been positive. If anything, I was still suffering from having a big head. I was bitter that my partners in the construction company had betrayed me. It would become clear to me later that the whole thing had been orchestrated by God, but for now, I was mad at them. I was also very much concerned about the spiritual direction of my life. I still had mountaintop spiritual experiences from time to time, but my normal spiritual temperature wasn't what I felt it should be. I had very little peace or joy in my life.

As I shared that concern with other Christian friends, I found that many of them were in the same place. When I was a new Christian, I went through a period of needing to know God better and I achieved that by waiting on God for every move I made. I was now in a similar position and had decided, that I wasn't going to look for a job, but I was going to wait on God to supply one. I was also going to start spending time with God each day and try to get back to where I was spiritually when Dina and I were first married. I didn't really need to work for a while because of my settlement with the construction company. But I didn't want to sit around and get rusty while I was waiting for God to send me my permanent new job, so I decided to do the lawns Mark and Robert had been doing during the summer.

Mark had already left to go back to college and Robert was only a few weeks away from leaving for the Navy. So, in October, I started mowing yards. I was terribly out of shape. I had to take two or three breaks to get through the first yard, but within a few months, I got to where I could finish five or six yards without a break.

I had a spiritual breakthrough in October as well. Our church was offering a course published by NavPress, entitled the *Colossians 2:7 Series*. It was a study of the fundamental biblical principles and disciplines of developing a strong relationship with God. It sounded exactly like what I was looking for, so both Dina and I signed up. That study changed my life. I began seriously practicing the disciplines that the course taught and the peace and joy that I hadn't experienced for years, once again returned.

Coincidentally, while we were studying a chapter on Biblical decision making, I was offered an amazing proposition to return to West Africa. A man offered to put up half a million dollars with no strings attached for me to go back and start a construction company that would be my own. If the company was successful, he wanted half of the profits, and if it failed, I didn't owe him anything. What a deal! I couldn't have asked for a better offer. But I was so excited about my newly revived relationship with God that I turned him down. Because I wanted to finish the course that I'd started to see where it would take me. I continued to feel stronger spiritually and that seemed to be helping our marriage as well.

Dina and I started going to counseling, which also helped, but something happened during the counseling that would become a major issue later. I felt a need to confess my infidelity in Africa to Dina, but the counselor wouldn't allow it. He said that he didn't think that Dina could deal with it. He and I discussed it several times because now that I was back walking with the Lord, I felt a strong conviction to confess it. But I ultimately yielded to his counsel and we moved on.

Things were getting kind of thin financially and I began to wonder if I'd made the right decision, but I held my course. Then, in February I received an offer from a neighbor to be a construction consultant for his accounting firm. The offer seemed interesting and the hourly fees were good, but it was only for about ten hours a week. His firm had a contract to oversee construction projects for a Government agency in Houston. They had approximately seven projects to be built and none of the people on the government staff or the accounting firm had construction experience. I wasn't getting very many hours at first, but as I began to point out problems in their construction accounting process, my billable hours began to climb. For example, there were no accountability measures in place to keep the builder from overbilling the government in his monthly draws. I helped them set up some basic schedules of values that had to be completed prior to payments and they were so excited about the results, they gave me more hours and a raise.

Within several months I had so much work with the firm that I had to start hiring a staff. By the time we had finished several of the buildings, the accounting firm realized they needed a maintenance team and asked me if I would like to handle that as well. I accepted, and they gave me a contract for maintenance of their buildings. I now had a 12-person staff and we were running like a clock. We were saving the government a bunch of money and making a bunch of money for ourselves. The only problem was that we were saving the government too much money and in government, if you don't use it, you lose it. I was not an insider, but I heard that when the government agency we worked for realized how much money they had saved by using our services, they started hiring consultants, so they could use the money up before the end of the fiscal year. Apparently, they were hiring friends and relatives for these positions and that didn't go over well when they were audited.

So the accounting firm I was working for and the government employee who had hired them were both put under serious scrutiny and ultimately relieved of their positions. We were asked by the accounting firm to please stop work and stand by until everything was resolved. They gave us money to cover payroll for a month, but things dragged on a lot longer than that. After the month they paid for ran out, I continued to pay our people in hopes that we would be reinstated. But we were deemed guilty by association and, we never got a chance to get our contract restored.

I spent almost all the profits on keeping our people on staff while things were in limbo. But God is faithful and came through I went back to mowing yards again. After a few months of that and dabbling briefly in a few other ventures, one of my old customers from my steel business, called and asked if I'd be interested in looking at a major hospital project in downtown Houston.

I don't know how I did it because I had no money, but I was awarded the contract and I was back in the steel business. I made a deal with a friend of mine to do the steel fabrication portion of the contract and I hired the workers directly to erect the steel. Before long I had several more contracts and once again we were doing well.

Before the hospital project was completed, I started having problems with my friend that was doing my fabrication. He said he was not making any money on the fabrication and he wanted to sever our relationship. I couldn't understand it because I knew the money I was paying him should have made the work very profitable for him. I found out later that his wife who was his office manager, while blaming the lack of money on me, was really stealing money from the company to fund her divorce and departure from my friend.

God used my separation from them to force me to open my own shop so that both the fabrication and erection of all our jobs were now being done by my own employees. It was 1994 and almost all the money we made had to be put back into the company to fund our growth, and at least on paper, we really began to prosper.

It was just Dina and Stacie and I at home now and although we didn't get along famously, Dina and I got along well enough and my relationship with Stacie was closer and stronger than ever. Just the opposite was the case with my daughter Lindsey. After my divorce from Jenny, she made it very difficult for me to see Lindsey. Lindsey was too young to fly by herself to Houston, so I had to visit her in Atlanta. That's a twelve-hour drive each way, so I only saw her a few times a year. I did call her regularly, and with my visits, I was able to maintain a reasonably close relationship with her. When she was six or seven, she was old enough to fly by herself, but her visits were very traumatic. While she knew me well, the rest of my family were total strangers to her. Even after she'd made several visits, it still didn't get any better. Almost every night, we would have to call Jenny before Lindsey could settle down and sleep. It tore me apart to watch Lindsey in such distress. I was angry with Jenny because I felt if she had honored the visitation guidelines of our divorce, Lindsey would have grown up knowing Dina and our children and her visits would have been far more enjoyable for her.

I was stressed about what to do because I didn't want Lindsey to continue to be so traumatized. Jenny had remarried and the man she married seemed to treat Lindsey well. And Lindsey seemed to accept him as a father figure. In light of all that, I wrote Jenny a letter telling her that first of all, I held her responsible for the problem of Lindsey feeling like a stranger in our home but offered to back out of her life and allow her new husband to bond with Lindsey until she got a little older. When I wrote the letter, I didn't intend it to be a final communication. I was hoping that it would open a dialog between Jenny and me to find a way to handle the situation in a way that would be best for Lindsey.

Unfortunately, I didn't hear back from Jenny. I waited and waited and heard nothing. Years later she told me she didn't respond because I had blamed her for the problem. I continued to send support, and presents on Christmas and birthdays, but heard nothing. Being a person who hated confrontations, I did the worst thing I could have done and that's nothing, I didn't hear from Jenny or Lindsey again until Lindsey was a junior in high school. One day I got a call from Lindsey asking to visit. I was excited to see her, and our relationship started all over again. Jenny had gotten divorced from her husband and I think she was freaking out that she might have to foot the bill for Lindsey's college. But, whatever the reason, I was happy to be reunited with Lindsey. I started visiting her again and she came to visit us in Houston. It was obvious that there were some problems in our relationship, which was understandable, but I was hoping we could work those out. Once again, I'll say, I was happy to see her again.

The Bible church where we'd been members was going through some changes. There was a new pastor who didn't really like the location of our church. It was in a declining neighborhood and He wanted to relocate to an up and coming area and to present a more relevant Gospel. We sold the church, lost quite a few of the members and started holding services and youth activities in a new planned community west of Houston. I don't remember the details, but before too long, we abandoned the new community, the pastor quit, and the core group of members that were left, ended up merging with another small group of believers and started meeting not too far from the former church site. It was in a better neighborhood though. We stayed with them for a while and helped with the reorganization of the group as a church.

I got to chair the committee assigned the task of rewriting our mission statement. That was an experience that opened my eyes to several things that I'd never realized. The newly appointed elders of the church gave our committee the mandate to write a mission statement that would steer the church to becoming like the first church described in Acts chapters two and four. When we were given the assignment, it seemed easy. But there's a big difference between writing down a description of what the early church looked like, and what it was that made them who they were. I spent a week, reading and rereading the first four chapters of Acts and praying for a clue as to why they were so close, why they shared everything they had and why they had so much power.

It finally dawned on me that they each had a like passion to share Christ with the world and that desire was more powerful than their own personal ambitions or survival. They had the power of the Holy Spirit to unite them, inspire them, empower them, direct them and propel them. But what made them who they were as a church was that sharing Christ with the world was a primary priority for each of them. Wow, and we wonder why the church is so weak today. That realization has become a milestone moment in my life's journey as a Christian.

I also became close with our new pastor. I spent a lot of time in prayer with him. We went on several short mission trips to the Mexican border, we went to two prayer and fasting conferences held by Bill Bright, founder and CEO of *Campus Crusade for Christ*. And on several occasions, we got together for all night prayer. He was a big encouragement to me in my spiritual struggles at home and in other areas of life. It seems like, from the moment of my salvation, God has always given me someone as a cheerleader and encourager in my journey.

I had been helping with Saturday night services at one of the local men's shelters for years, but after finishing the Colossians 2:7 series, I started teaching the series one afternoon a week at the shelter as well. I got so close with some of the men in my classes that I took several runs at starting a halfway house for some of them to move into. I think I got a little ahead of God on that, but I saw quite a bit of positive fruit in the lives of the guys I got involved with. The biggest thing I learned from those experiences is that *there is no shortcut to spiritual growth.* You can know and practice all the Christian disciplines, and those disciplines will help you and direct you on the journey, but *in order to grow and mature as believers, God has to take us through trials to refine us.* No human can design a path for spiritual growth. The more I study Psalm 139, the more I'm convinced that God has a special plan for each of us and only He knows the path to the fulfillment of that plan.

In October of 1998, I decided to get a bigger life insurance policy. Lindsey was in college and Stacie was getting close to her college years, so I thought it would be wise to get a better policy. The policy required a physical and since I had just had a full physical a month earlier, I figured it would not be a problem. I was wrong, I was turned down because my PSA level was slightly elevated. They told me that it might not be anything, but that I should get my prostate checked. I went to the doctor and he told me the level of my PSA was not high enough to be concerned but seeing the difference between my September and October physicals, as a precaution he wanted to get an ultrasound done within a few weeks. The ultrasound found nothing, but they took another PSA reading and it had climbed even more. The doctor knew something was not right, so he ordered biopsies. Five of the nine biopsies were malignant.

I was driving through Jack in the Box when the doctor called me and said, you have a problem. I don't think there's a more defining moment for any person than when you hear the words, YOU HAVE CANCER. I went numb for a few minutes, but came to my senses and thought, if I really believe what I say I believe about being a Christian, I can't let this shake me. I'd heard enough horror stories about chemotherapy to know that if they couldn't cure me through surgery, I was ready to die before I submitted to chemo.

So, I got my affairs in order, I closed out all my projects, I closed my steel company again and scheduled surgery for December 8th. It was a new procedure involving nerve grafts that were designed to produce a more natural recovery. The surgery took over eight hours and it didn't really do all that it was supposed to, but all my cancer appeared to be gone. Until my insurance PSA checkup in September, I had never had a prostrate physical. Then to have another one, thirty-days later had to be the hand of God. Either one of those tests by itself would not have alarmed anyone. But together they probably saved my life.

God continued to show his hand in my life. I had bid on a sizable railing restoration project several months before my bout with cancer and as soon as I had recovered from my surgery, the client called me to tell me they wanted to start the project. It was a sizable project, and somewhat dangerous, restoring approximately a mile and a half of balcony railing on a twenty-story condominium. The project took nearly a year to complete and turned out to be very profitable. That was all I needed to start a business up again and with an operation that was better than before. We won contracts for some major renovations at the Houston Intercontinental Airport and several other large projects.

The reorganized church we were members of didn't seem to be languishing, and the pastor left to take another position. Dina and I both started talking about looking for another church, so that's what we did. Since completing the 2:7 Series, my quiet times with God had grown to average between two and three hours each day and I was looking for a church with a strong spiritual ministry and a pastor whose leadership would challenge me.

We visited a Baptist church not too far from our house and immediately felt it was where God wanted us. We didn't join right away, but got involved gradually. The church had a strong focus on international ministry and a very diverse ethnic membership. We went on a mission trip to Monclova, Mexico and during the trip made the decision to join the church. After the trip, I began spending one-on-one time with the pastor and looking for some ways that I might get more involved with the church and its ministry. We discussed that although the church had a strong spiritual ministry, the church committee system was, for the most part, non-functional and several areas of the church's operation were beginning to suffer as a result.

The most serious need was the church facility itself. It had been a while since any maintenance had been done other than emergency repairs and there were numerous things in serious need of repair. I felt my gift was administration, and that with my construction background, God had prepared me and was calling me to get the facility back in proper working order. It took some time, but we organized and implemented a repair plan and developed a preventative maintenance program that seemed to please everyone.

Next, we discussed me chairing the Committee on Committees an oversight group that helped staff all the other committees. As I investigated the task ahead, we discovered that most of the church administration and training manuals were outdated and incorrect. The people of the church had been complaining that they weren't in the loop on decisions. It seemed to me that because the operation of the church had been turned over to the pastor and membership involvement had gradually deteriorated.

The pastor had a charismatic personality, and people were happy to give him a free hand to run the church. But it evolved into an unhealthy situation where the pastor was carrying most of the administrative load. As a result, almost all the training manuals needed editing, reprinting, and distribution. Once that was completed, which took several months, we began re-staffing all the committees.

I also started helping the pastor with the new member orientation classes and with the organization of mission trips. By this point, the pastor and I had become very close and we were working very effectively together. We had even talked about me becoming his administrator and managing the whole administrative side of the church. But before we got too far in implementing that, the church hired an assistant pastor and it was decided that he would handle many of the things we had talked about me doing. Honestly, I was a little offended that the plans were changed. The new assistant pastor was black and fit the ethnic mix of the church better than I did. So I didn't say anything and continued to help where ever I could.

As the committee situation improved, I began to focus more of my attention on missions. In 2000, I received an invitation from Victor, a Honduran missionary friend to visit a house church in the mountains of Honduras. I was told by Victor, that the people of that church had been praying for more than two years for someone to come and help them build a church building. I got the blessing of my pastor and went for a visit.

Victor told me they were in the mountains of Honduras, but that was an understatement. The town was approximately forty miles from Gracias, the town where Victor lived, and it took us nearly three hours to get there from Victor's home. The neat little village of La Union was populated by coffee farmers, most of whom lived in houses with dirt floors. There we met with the leaders of the church.

They served us lunch, then showed us the plot of land that they'd purchased for the church building and gave me an approximate budget of what they needed to construct the church building. I thoroughly enjoyed our meeting, but all I could think about during the trip back to Gracias and that night in the hotel was how could I bring a group of men and women up there? It would be a very challenging trip to get to La Union and once we got there, it would be like camping out.

Victor and I met again the next morning with Ross, a translator friend who had accompanied me on the trip. We had what I'll call a spirited conversation about whether our church should agree to help the church in La Union because I had objections primarily concerning the wellbeing of our church members. While Victor was trying to convince me that God was calling us to help, in the middle of the conversation, a tremendous peace about helping them overcame me, and I agreed to go back and present to my church the request I'd received from the church in La Union.

There was already a meeting scheduled for me to report about my trip so when I got off the plane in Houston on Sunday I went directly to the church meeting to share the experiences of the trip. When I finished my report, several members stood up and in tears stated that God had assured them that we needed to go and help the church in La Union. We sent the church in La Union the money required to finish the foundation of the church and scheduled a mission trip for the next summer. In 2001, I led a group from our church to begin the construction of the walls.

Stacie had graduated from high school the summer of 2000 and registered to start at Houston Baptist University in the fall. Our steel business continued to do well, so well that we started getting lines of credit at the bank. That was a big step of freedom, because prior to that, I had to depend on our own cash flow for payroll or fund it out of my personal funds, and my pockets weren't very deep. We had been specializing in projects that were difficult or challenging. That could be a challenging schedule, difficult design or a difficult location to maneuver on while doing the erection work. Almost all the projects where we were called on had some extra degree of difficulty and the more projects we completed, the more calls we got. For a while, we were turning down more projects than we accepted.

The new lines of credit also allowed me to hire a larger management staff and gave me more freedom in my schedule. We were doing well.

I used my new freedom and income to take more mission trips as well as vacations with the family. Our most memorable vacation was to New York City for the holidays. I wanted the kids to see New York at Christmas time, and to relive my favorite memories of my childhood there. We rented a pair of adjoining suites at the *Grand Central Hyatt*. We did all the things I'd done growing up and then some. We went to the Radio City Christmas show, visited the top of the Empire State Building, went to a show at NBC Studios and had dinner at the Rainbow Room.

That was an amazing experience for the kids and another example of God taking care of us. When we got off the elevator to the Rainbow Room, we saw what had to be 150 people waiting in line for a table. We started to turn around and leave, but before we could get back on the elevator, we heard, "is there a party of eight in line?" We were the only party of eight and were seated immediately. What a blessing, and what a vacation.

My family and I continued to go on mission trips to Mexico and got comfortable making the trip. We also started looking at making some trips to Africa.

We returned to La Union in 2002 to finish the church walls and we also brought some of our church youth group on that trip. We held a program at the high school where our students gave their Christian testimonies and the local senior class students shared their plans. I was thoroughly impressed by the details and enthusiasm of their plans. At the end of the program, I asked the La Union students if they had the means to follow through on their dreams for the future. One by one they hung their heads and said no. It broke my heart. It was apparent that they had spent a serious amount of time thinking and dreaming about the future to come up with the plans they shared. And to see that they had no opportunity to follow through was purely heartbreaking. It was that incident that God used to show me how badly those kids needed hope.

By the summer of 2003, we were on our third church mission trip to La Union and we were putting the roof on the church building. Even though it still didn't have windows or doors, I considered my work there complete. I had begun saying my goodbyes, but on the morning before we were scheduled to leave, I heard the Holy Spirit say, "You're not finished here yet."

As you can imagine, I was a bit stunned. Without knowing any Spanish, I struggled to construct a church, and now God was telling me there was more. At the time I heard the Holy Spirit, I was standing on the street in front of the church dorm where we had stayed and replied, "If there's something else you want me to do, you at least have to give me someone who speaks English, so I can ask some questions." As soon as I finished those words, a young lady walked up to me and said, "Good Morning". Her name was Vanessa. I had seen her before, but didn't know she spoke English. I asked her if she spoke English and she said: "yes, I'm the only one in town that speaks English".

Overwhelmed by such an immediate answer to prayer, I sat down on the curb and began to weep. She asked me why I was weeping, and I told her what I had just prayed. Then she began to weep. I asked her why she was weeping, and she said that she had just prayed that God would glorify himself by using her English. Then we both sat on the curb and wept together. We talked for a while, but I didn't really get any insights into what God might want me to do, but it was clear that there was still something more that God wanted me to do in La Union.

Chapter Nineteen
My Calling to La Union?

On the plane ride back to Houston, I sat next to a girl who could have been a PR spokesperson for bilingual schools in Honduras. She told me that her parents had been active on the governing board of the bilingual school she had just completed. She was on her way to start college in San Antonio and quoted every statistic imaginable about how students with a bilingual education excel in comparison to students without a bilingual education.

By the time we arrived in Houston, I couldn't help but think that maybe God wanted me to start a bilingual school in La Union. Somewhere between my time of weeping on the curb with Vanessa and now, God had communicated to me that His calling for me had to do with bringing hope to the youth of La Union. Before I left La Union, I learned of an effort by Vida Abundante Church to start a bilingual school for the wealthier children of La Union, I thought maybe God wanted me to open a school for the poorer children who couldn't afford the other school. I made several trips back to La Union over the next year to investigate the feasibility of a second bilingual school. On each trip, I felt the undeniable presence of God in my meetings and travel. I once again prayed intensely, putting out fleece after fleece as I did when I left my steel company partner in 1985, looking for God's confirmation and seemed to always receive it.

Some of the confirmation experiences were unmistakable and unforgettable. For example, before each trip, I would make sure that I had a translator to travel with me while I was in Honduras. On one trip at the last minute, my translator had to back out. So, as I got on the plane in Houston, I was frantic. I started asking people on the plane if they knew anyone that could travel with me as a translator during my four-day journey through Honduras. I found no one. So, I prayed. "Lord, if you really want me to follow through with this bilingual school, you're going to have to have a translator waiting for me when I arrive in Honduras."

When I got off the plane, I went to the car rental counter to rent a car. Before I even asked about my car, I asked if the young lady at the counter knew anyone available to travel and translate for me during my four-day visit. She knew of a young man named Eric, who was about to get off from one of the other car rental companies and he would probably do it. Sure enough, he agreed, and my prayers had been answered. Things like that happened on every trip. Because God had provided so much encouragement and affirmation, I finally decided to start a one-year free bilingual school to see what the results would be. I hired Jenny, a bilingual teacher who had been teaching in San Pedro Sula, Honduras and bought a curriculum package. In August of 2004, we started with twenty students. We were amazed to see how well the children did.

Within only a few months some of the students were scoring nearly perfect grades on their progress tests. I must add that because we had not yet become an accredited school, these children were attending public school in the morning for six hours and then attending our school in the afternoon for another four hours. I was also amazed at the hunger to learn that our kids displayed.

One incident illustrating their hunger to learn had such an impact, that I still tell about it to this day. One of our best students, a young man named Geovany, I think he was about nine or ten, came to school one day soaking wet. It wasn't raining, so we asked him how he got so wet. As it turns out, that there is a large creek or small river that runs between his house, (an approximate 30-minute walk away) and our school. There was no bridge over the creek and it had rained the night before, so the water level was up.

But rather than miss school, when Geovany reached the creek, he removed his clothes and waded through the waist-deep, rushing water of the creek, carrying his clothes over his head and put his clothes back on when he reached the other side. When he told us the story, all I could think about was myself as a boy. I didn't skip much school, but I couldn't even imagine that I or any of my friends would ever dream of doing something like that.

During the first year, we held classes in the back of the Baptist church we had built. We also purchased property next to it and began to expand the 800 square foot house into a facility that would eventually become a mission base for beginner missionaries. We had several visits from Houston churches to help us construct a better classroom environment in the church and help with the construction of the mission base. It appeared that we were on course in the fulfillment of our calling in La Union.

After completing that first year, both Jenny and I felt that with the success we had, we needed to try at least one more year. We felt that we should commit to another year with the students we had and add another class of new students. Our biggest challenge in doing that was adding our classes to the public school schedule. If Jenny taught two four-hour classes our school wouldn't be getting out until 10:00 PM. So, to add a class, we would have to add another teacher. We faced another problem. I had been covering all the costs of the school out of my steel business in Houston and adding another class would almost double the cost of supporting the school. We had been getting some help from my church in Houston, but my business paid for most of it. I was a little concerned about taking on the additional commitment, but God had been blessing our efforts this far, so we assumed He would continue to do so.

So we moved forward with plans for adding a second class. As we began our search for a new teacher, we found out that one of my daughters Stacie's friends had just finished college and was looking for a job situation like what we had. So, without a lot of thought, we added Julie to our staff and acknowledged it as a provision of God. We decided to let Julie teach the second-year students and Jenny would take the new first-year students. We started year two, adding an additional twenty or so students. I think we had a total of about 44. My business was doing well in Houston and although like any new venture, we had some problems as the school grew, we progressed there as well.

Things were going so well in Honduras that I was beginning to feel like God wanted me and Dina to move to La Union full time. We talked about it a lot, but she was not at all interested.

Then in early 2006, I was approached by an architect on Roatan, an island off the coast and a part of Honduras and he asked me if I would be interested in building houses for him on Roatan. He had been told by a mutual friend that I had owned and managed a major home building company in Africa. At the time, he was designing and building homes and wanting to turn the construction portion of his business over to someone else. I thought it was an interesting idea, for no other reason than it would allow me to hire workers from La Union to work in Roatan, and I could disciple them in the process. As fate or God's planning would have it, there was a young man that I'd been working with in Houston named Ian, who had read an article in a newspaper about my venture in Africa and had been asking me if we could start a business together. When I told him about the offer in Roatan, he was ready. So, I met with Don the architect and reached what seemed to be a reasonably good arrangement, and although I was also ready in my mind, there were a lot of things I needed to consider.

I don't remember whether I even consulted Dina. We had become so far apart, we didn't agree on anything, and besides, I was only approaching the new business as a trial to see if the venture worked. Ian was going to run it and I would continue to travel back and forth between Houston and Honduras. The only difference was that my stays in Honduras would be longer.

My biggest consideration was what to do about my steel business? It was doing well, and we were well in the black by major six figures. But should I sell it or keep it and let someone else run it in my absence? My assistant manager had been with me for several years and she was very sharp, but we were regularly butting heads about some of the business fundamentals. She was an MBA graduate and was constantly champing at the bit to apply her business school education to make changes in the way we did things.

I could never get her to understand that we were not a Fortune 500 company nor was I interested in becoming one. And as I learned when I was attending business classes in college, they teach fundamentals that are designed for larger companies. When you are a small business, like we were with only 35 employees, there is no need or funding for outside consultants except in isolated cases.

But she was convinced that I was wrong. And that we needed consultants. For example, before hiring her, I had always run the business out of a spiral notebook and could tell you at any time within a few dollars where we were financially. I let her talk me into buying an expensive accounting program for our computers. It was complicated and not a fit for a company of our size. As I understood it, the only time she could tell me our financial status, was at the end of a quarter, and even then, I didn't feel we got as accurate an account as I could produce with my spiral notebook. But despite that, I decided to leave the business in her hands.

In May of 2006, we were off to build houses in Roatan and planned to disciple our workers for Christ.

Chapter Twenty
Moral Failure

With the heart of an entrepreneur and the enthusiasm of a new venture to start up, I was pretty much unstoppable, or so I thought. I had the blessing of my church, and felt I had the blessing of God, so what could stop me? Before I left Houston, after a last effort to convince Dina to join me, she responded with the statement, "I don't doubt that God is calling us to Honduras, but I'm not going!" That was another turning point in our relationship, but it wouldn't become obvious for a while. You would think that her statement would have taken the wind out of my sails, and it did have an effect, but you would have never known it by watching me over the next several months.

My plan was to organize a work crew in La Union of fourteen men and a cook then transport them to Roatan. We would then set up housekeeping for the group there and begin building houses. Ian, who was fluent in Spanish, would orchestrate the actual construction portion of the venture and I would take care of facilitating everything else. My job was to keep the living quarters stocked with food and operating efficiently. I had to deliver the hot lunches to the workers and I was also responsible for getting construction materials to the job sites.

When it was time to get started, I hired our workers in La Union and transported them to Roatan a week before Ian arrived. That sounds simple, but it was far from it.

Before transporting the entire crew, I took a few along with the cook to get set up. I rented a four-room house in Roatan that would serve as the crew's living quarters and bought some basic kitchen appliances. We built wooden bed frames for the foam mattresses that I bought in San Pedro Sula. I also leased an apartment for Ian and me to live in. Leaving the first group in Roatan to finish set-up preparations, I went back to get the remaining dozen workers, which in itself became an experience of a lifetime.

I had a rented double cab pick-up truck and loaded me and twelve men with their tools and luggage. I still didn't know any Spanish and they knew no English. We set out at 5:00 AM for a six-hour drive to La Ceiba, a coastal town where we would be catching a ferry for the twenty-five-mile ride to Roatan. The last ferry left at 3:30 PM. We knew we would have to stop for breakfast and bathroom breaks, so there was no time to waste. The drive went pretty well other than the challenge of trying to organize breakfast at Burger King in El Progresso. Getting the men in, seated and fed using sign language had to be an amusing sight for anyone watching. Many of these guys had never been to the city, let alone to an American style fast food restaurant. But it went well.

It was a very quiet ride, no one said much of anything. I didn't know if they were afraid or if that was just their culture. I later learned that most of the men had never heard of Roatan, and some of them even thought we were going to the United States.

We made it to the ferry station without any major problems, but there the circus was about to begin. I had to explain to them that they had to sit in the station and wait for me while I went to downtown La Ceiba to return our rented truck. I'm not sure whether they understood me, but once I got them seated, I think they were all too scared to move.

Buying breakfast at Burger King wasn't all that difficult. All I had to do was say "give me twelve number ones". But trying to buy a late lunch/early dinner in the ferry station's cafeteria for twelve men who had never been in a cafeteria, or even a normal restaurant was a much bigger challenge. Don't forget, I couldn't speak Spanish, so I couldn't communicate with the restaurant staff either. Finally, I stood up in the restaurant and shouted, "Does anyone here speak English?"

Fortunately, there was a young bi-lingual student about sixteen years old who stood up and said she could help. By this time the station was filled with a capacity ferry load of about 250 people, and they were all watching us. Everyone seemed to be enjoying the show. We got everyone fed, tickets purchased, and everyone loaded on the ferry. And fortunately, Anna, our new-found translator, offered to help us the rest of the way.

I've been dwelling on the challenges of the trip, but there were also many blessings. I watched wonderment on the men's faces as they saw the multistory buildings and the lighted signboards of San Pedro Sula and then the ocean for the first time. To see a whole new world open to these guys was indescribable. Most of them looked awestruck as they watched the waters of the Caribbean pass during the two and one-half hour ferry ride. I would have given anything to be able to have read their thoughts.

The fun began again once we reached Roatan. I had arranged for the long-term rental of a similar double cab pickup for our transportation on the island. Like before we maxed it out and then some. We must have been a sight. I learned later that it was against local laws to haul as many people as we did, but somehow, we got away with it.

We got everyone to the apartment without incident and our cook had supper ready for us as planned. So, as I headed to my apartment for the night, I was feeling pretty good. I had given the workers the next day off to get settled and get familiar with their new surroundings. Ian arrived that day and we were ready to go.

Or so I thought. That next morning Ian and I went to meet with Don, our architect partner, only to find out that he wasn't ready for us to start. He took us on a tour of all his current and future projects and it quickly became obvious to me that this guy was living in the future. I recognized it because that's how I used to live, living on the adrenaline of all the big potential things in the future. And from my many experiences, I had learned that you can get yourself in trouble living like that. If you spend all your efforts preparing for the future, you get in trouble in the present.

So, I readily understood why he wasn't ready for us. We had a very candid and frank conversation, after which he promised he would have work for us in a few days. A few days turned out to be a week, but at least we were finally underway. Something else he didn't tell us was that even though we were on an island, the sub-division we were going to build, was also on an island. Another island. So, we were going to build two houses on an island that required us to purchase building materials, haul them to a private dock for sub-division residents, load the materials onto a barge, wait for a driver to tow the barge to our building site then unload the materials at the site. That's not what we'd planned for, but we adapted and were finally working.

Despite all the extra work, we began to progress. Don and everyone else who was watching our operation were impressed. Our quality was better, and our progress was quicker than the local workers. I don't know if it was the fact that our workers were more skilled, our management was better, or it was just the laid-back attitude of the island workers, but we were out producing the locals in noticeable fashion. That made us feel good about our future on Roatan.

I started taking our crew to church and it was quickly obvious that even though the workers told me they were Christians, they weren't really interested in going to church. They went, but I could tell that, for the most part, it was only because they felt it was a requirement. After a few lackluster visits to church, I decided that discipleship was something that we would have to ease our way into. I learned a Milestone Lesson, that being that you can't develop a Christian discipleship ministry with non-believers or even less than enthusiastic believers no matter what the benefits of participation. Hunger for God can only be established by God.

We were doing well with the house construction, but I knew that, in order to turn a profit, we needed to have enough work to expand our crew from fourteen to twenty and keep them busy. I had told that to Don from the outset and he had assured me that was where we were headed. But it didn't take long before it became obvious that unless some new work fell from the sky, Don was going to be lucky to keep the original crew of fourteen busy. From a positive perspective, Ian had done a great job organizing the crew and our guys worked circles around the Roatan island workers.

With the combination of our crew being better than anyone had expected and Don's dreaming not becoming a reality, Ian and I decided that we needed to start looking for other work for the crew. I looked almost full time and Ian would help after construction hours. Because of the focus on looking for new business, I started slipping into some bad habits.

I guess it started with me not doing things that I should have done. Our days began really early. Because of the hot climate, we would start construction early and quit early to avoid heat-related problems for the workers. So, my morning quiet times were reduced from several hours to eventually only a few minutes. I went from a seriously extended time of reading my Bible and praying, which I had been doing faithfully every day for over ten years, to spending only a few minutes reading a devotional.

The early schedule wasn't the only problem. Ian and I were going out to eat almost every night and having a few drinks with the dinner. We weren't carousing, but that routine took its toll on my ability to get up early enough to practice the spiritual disciplines that had helped turn my life around. It didn't happen overnight, but before long I started making some stupid decisions.

Being out and about as much as I was, I started being friendlier than I should have been with some of the local girls, and eventually, I became intimate with several young ladies in their twenties. That only lasted a few weeks. I came to my senses quickly and started heading my life back in a better direction, but the damage was done. I had been unfaithful, something that I hadn't done since my time in Africa fourteen years earlier.

By August, we still hadn't landed any definite work and Don's work was dwindling. It was becoming clear that this venture was not going to work out as we had hoped. In mid-August, we started formulating an exit plan and by Labor Day, we shut down and went home. That was bad news enough, but it would get worse. The steel business in Houston was in trouble as well. As I said earlier, it was hard for the accounting software we were using to see where you were at any given moment. I had still been keeping my own monthly spiral notebook ledger, and even though my manager told me it wasn't as bad as I thought, my notebook bookkeeping convinced me that the business was in trouble.

I made some dramatic decisions. I knew that without the steel company, there could be no school. So, when I returned to La Union, I shut down the bilingual school, sent the teachers home, put all the furniture, equipment and housewares in storage and headed back to Houston to see what could be done to save the sinking steel business.

It didn't take long to figure out that it would take a miracle to turn the business around, and with the guilt I carried because of my behavior on Roatan, I wasn't expecting any favor from God. After evaluating our payables and receivables I decided to visit customers to tell them we were shutting down. I had built strong relationships with several our customers and they responded with grace and compassion. After they were convinced that there was no turning around the company, all but one helped me by paying all the outstanding invoices they owed. I started selling our equipment, tools and other assets using the funds to begin settling accounts with our suppliers. After liquidating our assets and paying what I could, I was still $250,000 in debt. I had a good relationship with most of my creditors and even though I wasn't sure how I was going to do it, I promised to make good on all our debts.

How do you pay off a quarter of a million dollars in debt with no job and no company? It was obvious that I had to get a job, but I hadn't been employed in 25 years. I didn't have any work references and I really wondered if anyone would give a job to a guy who had just closed his business. And I wasn't just looking for just any job. It needed to be paid well enough to pay off a minimum of $6,000 a month in interest on my debts, plus my living expenses. Despite having little hope, I set out to see what I could find.

I approached one of my creditors, who was also a competitor and one of our steel suppliers. We had done a lot of work together and I asked the general manager if I could use him as a job reference. He said sure and asked what kind of position I was looking for. I knew him well enough to lay my cards on the table. To my surprise, he offered me a job with his company. I told him what I needed to make, and he agreed. So, on the Monday after Thanksgiving Day of 2006, I became a project manager for a major steel fabrication company.

The company had just reorganized and had created a new position that I was filling. Prior to that time, the sales people had been managing their own projects, but they wanted the salespeople to focus on sales, so I took over the management of approximately forty projects. Some were small, but the majority were large projects. In the first week, I was handed the information for all the active projects and I must admit I was overwhelmed. I consider myself a talented project manager of steel fabrication projects, but I was overwhelmed. One person, no matter how talented, cannot effectively manage forty projects at a time, but I was hoping to keep up with them well enough until I could work them into a manageable flow. I didn't want to tell my new boss that the task was impossible, and I didn't want to complain. So, I dug in my heels, rolled up my sleeves, put my head down and got to work.

It was the most difficult assignment I had ever undertaken. There were endless emails, the phone was constantly ringing and there was always a line of people at my door. But, I got the job done and, in my opinion, I did it well. My effectiveness was acknowledged by others as well, we began getting compliments from our sister company employees and customers that I had made a noticeable improvement in our company's project management. It was extremely difficult, but one good thing was, they didn't expect me to work unreasonable hours to keep up. I came in at 7:00 AM, took an hour for lunch and went home at 4:30 PM. I worked my butt off during the time I was there, but when I was off, I was off.

Christmas came and went, and I started the New Year with a new anticipation. It was going to be a long, tough haul, but it looked like there was hope again. I felt like someday I may be able to be out of debt. But something happened the first week of 2007 that once again, rocked me to the core.

Chapter Twenty-One
Almost at the Bottom

I thought I was at the bottom, but little did I know it was going to get worse, a lot worse.

The first Sunday in January of 2007, I was at church with Dina and Stacie and towards the end of the sermon, I had the strongest conviction about sin that I think I'd ever had. I don't think it had anything to do with the sermon, but suddenly I was reminded of all my infidelity during my time in Africa and in Roatan. It was all I could think about. I didn't say anything at the time, but by that afternoon, I felt I had to confess. I called my pastor and told him of my conviction and confessed my various infidelities both in Africa and on Roatan. I also told him that before I told anyone else, I needed to confess to my family.

At this point, Dina and I had been married nearly 26 years. I'd been for the most part miserable in the marriage, which is no excuse for infidelity, but I felt like God was saying it's time for me to confess all the infidelity issues in my life and begin to look at solutions. I had had my times of total disobedience to my marital vows when I was in Africa and Roatan, but to my thinking, (which I know was wrong), if I didn't kiss another woman on the mouth or have sex, I was behaving myself. In past years, I had been convicted by God's Spirit and I had confessed several close calls of incidents of near intimacy to my pastor. So, although this wasn't a totally new behavior, this time was different. It was like God wanted to do a total house cleaning in me.

I told Dina the next day, and she went ballistic. I hadn't expected anything less, and I know I deserved it, but all the same, it was awful. Although our marriage had been bad, I felt a certain level of guilt towards her, our marriage had been so bad that my primary guilt came from the fact that I had disgraced God.

Next, I needed to confess to my children, primarily Stacie. She thought I was Superman. By now she was married and living in Ft. Worth with her husband Mitch. I remember as I was making that four-hour drive to confess and apologize to her, I was so depressed. As I drove, I remember looking for places along the freeway where I might be able to stage a suicide on the way back in a way that I could make look like a legitimate accident.

Dina had already told Stacie why I was coming, so it wasn't a surprise, but I remember hugging her and begging her to forgive me as I cried uncontrollably. I obviously didn't commit suicide on the back, but I think I did cry most of the way. Stacie was devastated. I had been her hero and we were extremely close. The one thing she said that made me feel worst of all, was that she didn't know what she could believe about me anymore.

I met with my pastor the day after I told Stacie, and although my confession had obviously affected our relationship, he treated me with respect and I even felt his compassion. We had become close friends and had done a lot together on behalf of the church. The meeting was very difficult for both of us. I had written a confession detailing every act of infidelity that I could remember committing. I also made a point of resigning from every position I had with our church. He asked me to do two things. First, that I would get started in counseling and secondly, I would make an oral confession to the trustees and deacons of the church. I immediately made an appointment for counseling and went to my first session the next week. So, by the time I met with the church leadership, counseling was underway. Just before the meeting, the pastor and I met to pray, and I remember him saying to me as we left for the meeting, "I'm with you in this." When he said that I sensed a peace, but it didn't last long.

As the pastor had requested, I began an oral confession to the church leadership. I was so emotional I worried that I might break down crying, so I tried to speak in a monotone or unemotional tone. That was probably a mistake because I think they misinterpreted that to mean that I was unrepentant. When I was finished there was a discussion but I don't really remember what was said. I do remember that it seemed very hostile. What I remember most is that about halfway through the discussion, the pastor had a total change of countenance. He went from being supportive to becoming an attacker. I never understood why he changed, and I guess it doesn't matter.

I never expected to be treated well, but I was surprised at how hostile most of them were. I wasn't caught doing wrong, but had confessed it, I felt that I had followed a scriptural path since being convicted by the Holy Spirit, and because I had already started counseling, I thought that my friends, which many of them were, would have been more civil. There were one or two who spoke up on my behalf, but they were quickly silenced.

Although what I had done was inexcusable, I feel like the response of the leadership was far from biblical. Before the meeting was over, without any prayer or further discussion, several deacons went before the attendees of the early church service (which was underway as we were meeting), to declare my wrongs and to announce that I'd been removed from the deacon board.

I'm not trying to portray myself as a saint being wronged, my actions of infidelity were horrible, but I felt like my actions since the time of my initial confession were motivated by my concern for the church and a desire to minimize damage that may have been caused by my sins to the body of believers. At that time, I was highly visible and respected as a church leader. I wanted to apologize to the members in a way that put the blame on me and to try to do it in a way that would glorify God. It seemed like all the leadership was interested in doing was to destroy me in the eyes of the members. I think it could have been handled a lot better and I think that the spiritual damage to the members could have been minimized had there been more prayer. I think the entire Bible is about reconciliation, but that didn't seem to be the intention of the leadership.

I left the meeting in tears, never to return to the church. I don't understand the actions of the leadership, but I'd come to the point of knowing that nothing can happen to me except with God's permission. And as time passed it became obvious that God's future path for me had to take me through that experience to get me where

He eventually wanted me to be. But for now, I was devastated and was sure that there was no place for me, but life's dung pile. And I was no longer fit for God's service. Almost all my personal friends had disowned me, and I was seriously in debt. It was a lonely place to be. But God used that time to really turn my life around. It would be a very wide turn, one that would take several years.

Even though I was in a state of depression, I knew the fundamental things I needed to do to keep from making things worse. I immediately started attending another church. I had heard that a Christian radio teacher that I had listened to and supported in previous years, had moved to Houston and was pastoring a church nearby. I visited, and it became obvious to me after just one service that it was the place God wanted me to be. The first time I attended was amid a Bible conference that met several times during that week. I tried to keep a low profile, but during one of the meetings, the speaker asked that everyone to break up into groups of three for prayer. I wanted to leave, but before I could, two men, Robert and Ada, grabbed me and asked me to join them. I only remember that they had the discernment to know I was hurting. I felt I didn't have a choice but to tell them about my situation and we began to pray. I don't remember anything earthshaking happening that night, but I now had friends at the church and because of that, I began to feel a part of it. Robert and I went on to become good friends.

I knew that I needed to tell the leadership of this new church about my situation before they heard about me from someone else, so I made an appointment with the pastor. In my meeting with the pastor, I did my best to explain my situation and asked if he would be my representative in trying to reconcile the hostile exit from my previous church. I was not interested in returning as a member, but wanted to apologize to the church membership and ask their forgiveness. He promised he would. I never saw the emails between him and the previous pastor, but he said he got a very hostile response that offered no hope for reconciliation. The pastor told me after some time that the previous pastor had sent him a follow-up response asking him to reconsider allowing me to even be a part of the new church.

I continued to get involved in the new church, Encourager Church, and eventually became a member. There were several members at Encourager that I'd known in the past. Three of them I knew very well. Patrick and Carrie Richardson were former neighbors of mine, and they were friendly and familiar faces. Another was a minister from the inner city whom I had helped to start a Christian youth football league. It was now a thriving program. I didn't realize it at the time, but he told me that I had been the first major donor to the program. That was an encouragement when I needed it most. I also found that Wally Wood and his wife were members. He's the man I mentioned earlier who had devoted his life to the study of the end times. Being reunited with Wally offered some stability in my journey back to being reconciled as a part of God's family, but I had a long way to go.

Dina and I tried to get back to normal, but unfortunately normal was even more challenging than before. All the kids were grown and gone, it was just her and me.

I was also making a very unpleasant commute to work every day. An hour plus in the morning, which wasn't too bad because I listened to Bible teaching on the Christian radio station, but the evening commute was torture. The drive time was about the same, but after a day's work in my new project manager position, I was spent, and the anticipation of an evening of less than cordial conversation was very depressing. Once again, I'm not saying I didn't deserve punishment for my actions, but Dina found it difficult to forgive me and to me, it appeared, that she was more interested in the opportunity to rub my nose in it. We went to counseling together doing the assigned reconciliation exercises, but it didn't seem to be going anywhere.

By April, after a lot of prayer about the situation, I decided to move out and get an apartment a few blocks from my job. I felt like God had given me a one-year reconciliation plan to present to Dina, but at the time she didn't want to discuss it. So, on the first weekend in April, which also happened to be our twenty-sixth anniversary weekend, I moved out. I didn't plan it that way, but when you move, you normally move at the beginning of the month.

Living by myself, I remember being very lonely and depressed. My job beat me up nine hours a day. I felt like a vegetable by the time I left in the afternoon, but even so, I considered it a blessing. It kept me so busy during the day that I didn't have time to think about anything else but my work. In the evening, I was so tired I didn't want to think about anything. It was a simple life. I would walk around the apartment complex in the early evening, eat supper, watch a little TV then go to bed. I would get up early in the morning and have several hours of quiet time, then go to work. During my quiet times, I would primarily read my Bible and other Christian literature, mixed with meditation and prayer. Saturdays and Sundays were pretty much spiritual days when I would try to focus my time and attention on spiritual things. I would go to church on Sunday mornings and Wednesday evenings. That was my life.

Prior to my moral failure, I always had been on the move. My schedule was packed because I had my family and business. When the kids were growing up, we always went to their school activities, plays, football games and pretty much anything that parents were invited to. We would take several extended weekend vacations per year, and we went on camping trips in the spring and fall. After the older ones had moved out on their own, we had regular family get-togethers for meals.

Business kept me busy as well, I would regularly put in ten to twelve-hour days, not because I had to, but because I enjoyed what I did. Besides family and business, I was always busy with church activities and other commitments. I was heavily involved in our sub-division homeowners association. I was active in politics, a precinct chairman for the Republican Party and an election judge. That sounds like a lot, and it is, but I always seemed to have time for everything. My schedule was always full. So, it was a major adjustment to get used to this new schedule, but once again, I considered it a blessing. The new schedule gave me a lot of time for spiritual reading, prayer, meditation, and reflection.

God really taught me a lot during this time. I think the biggest thing I learned, was what salvation was about. In the early years of being a Christian, it wasn't long before I understood the difference between works and faith. If someone asked me why I was going to heaven, I would say and believe that it was because I had accepted Jesus Christ as my Savior. That was what I believed, and I thought that's what most Christians believed. But I found out that was not the case.

In the eighties, I was part of a church program that went out into our community with intentions of leading people to Christ. We went door to door introducing ourselves as being from the local church, then we would start with a survey. The first question we asked was, "Do you think you're going to heaven when you die?" Most people said, "Yes." The second question was, "If God asked you why He should let you into heaven, what would you say?" I was amazed at how many answered that it was because they thought they were a pretty good person. I remember that *less than 10%* of the people we talked to said that God would let them into Heaven because they had accepted Christ as their Savior. (The correct answer.)

I am telling you, the reader, this to make a point. Although I realized that the "pretty good person" response was incorrect during the survey, after my moral failure, I came to realize that although I knew the right answer to the survey question, I had come to trust more in my good works than in the sin sacrifice of Jesus. I say that because, after my moral failures, I had no good works to rely on for my inner peace concerning my salvation. I had come to a point where I thought my life was worth little more than a contribution to life's dung pile. Because of that, I began to doubt my salvation and had to learn all over again that my salvation had nothing to do with my good works for God but came only from accepting the sin sacrifice of our Lord Jesus Christ.

Now that my good works had been erased, and I could see nothing but bad within me, I had to find peace about my salvation solely in the fact that I had accepted Christ as my Savior and in His work on the cross. I know that probably sounds like a simple concept, but when your conviction of sin is at the level that mine was, it's hard to comprehend God's love to be big enough for that amount of forgiveness. Now all I had was God's promise. All I had to stand on was God's promise of salvation through Christ. It took me several months to get my mind around that and be able to stand on God's salvation promise and nothing else. To be able to say that with confidence, was the beginning of seeing God's word the Bible and its promises in a totally new light. All, of God's promises, His love, His grace and His patience took on a whole new life and meaning for me. I would begin a more genuine life of faith.

As soon as I had moved into my new apartment, I began reading and recording God's promises one by one all over again. I found an entry in my journal from early April that said, "I have to keep convincing myself that God still loves me. I feel like I have let him down so badly, I feel so unworthy of His forgiveness." Somehow, those thoughts encouraged me, because I know that those were the thoughts of a repentant heart.

The remainder of 2007 was devoted to reconnecting with God on a new faith-based foundation. As I review my journal, I see that until the beginning of February 2008, there were a lot of spiritual ups and downs. It was a time of intense spiritual growth, and I feel like I should share some of the journal entries, especially the promises of God that energized the process of relearning scripture and how it helped me reconnect with God.

Journal Entries From 2007

Promise #1

As I listened to Charles Stanley's radio message yesterday, and he recited Proverbs 3:5-6 which says: *"Trust in the Lord with all your heart and lean not on your own understanding, in all your ways acknowledge Him and He will make your paths straight."*...I felt the tug of God's spirit saying, "That's your first promise,"

If I believe in the sovereignty and all-encompassing sufficiency of God, (which I do), if my life is based on that foundation verse, (promise), He can and will take me where He wants me to go. How can I fear that? How can I even be uncomfortable with that? How can I draw anything but peace and anticipation from that?

Promise #2

This is such a simple verse that I memorized long ago, but it never came to mind until my counselor mentioned it. 1 John 1:9 says: *"If we confess our sins, He is faithful and just, and will forgive us our sins and purify us from all unrighteousness."* It's the most comforting verse or promise that I've heard since this nightmare started.

Promise #3

This has been one of my anchoring passages for a long time concerning spiritual growth and maturity. 2 Peter 1:3-4 says: *"His divine power has given us everything we need for life and godliness through our knowledge of Him who called us by His own glory and goodness. Through these, He has given us His very great and precious promises, so that through them you may participate in the divine nature and escape the corruption in the world caused by evil desires."*

Promise #4

This is the first promise God revealed to me when I first became a Christian. I've come back to this passage and its foundational promise more than any other passage in scripture during my journey as a believer. Matthew 6:31-33 says: *"So do not worry, saying, What shall we eat? or What shall we drink? or What shall we wear? For the pagans run after these things and **your heavenly Father knows that you need them.** But seek first His kingdom and His righteousness, and all these things will be given you as well."* My financial well-being is God's responsibility.

Promise #5

I believe God showed me this verse as an amplifier to the previous passage. Hebrews 11:6 says: *"And without faith, it is impossible to please God, because anyone who comes to Him must believe that He exists and that He rewards those who earnestly seek Him."*

God went on for the rest of the year, giving me promise after promise from His Word. I stopped numbering them after twenty-nine, but He used those promises to convince me that my strength was not based on my confidence in my good works for God, but solely on the power of His promises. Here are a few more of them that strengthened me in my journey to reconciliation.

Romans 8:38-39, *"For I am convinced that neither death, nor life, neither angels nor demons, neither the present nor the future, nor any powers, neither height nor depth, nor anything else in all creation, will separate us from the love of God that is in Christ Jesus our Lord."*

Philippians 1:6, *"Being confident of this, that He who began a good work in you will carry it on to completion until the day of Christ Jesus."*

Jeremiah 29:11, *"For I know the plans I have for you, declares the Lord, plans to prosper you and not to harm you, plans to give you hope and a future."*

Joshua 1:8, *"Do not let this Book of the Law depart from your mouth, meditate on it day and night, so that you will be careful to do everything written in it, then you will be prosperous and successful."*

Matthew 10:29-31, *"Are not two sparrows sold for a penny? Yet not one of them will fall to the ground apart from the will of your Father. And even the very hairs of your head are all numbered. So, don't be afraid; you are worth more than many sparrows."*

Romans 3:22-23, *"This righteousness from God comes through faith in Jesus Christ to all who believe. There is no difference because all have sinned and fall short of the glory of God."*

Philippians 3:9, *"and be found in Him, not having a righteousness of my own that comes from the law, but that which is through faith in Christ-the righteousness that comes from God and is by faith."*

Psalm 89:30-33, *"If my sons forsake my law and do not follow my statutes, if they violate my decrees and fail to keep my commands, I will punish their sin with the rod, their iniquity with flogging;* **but I will not take my love from him nor will I ever betray my faithfulness."**

As I said earlier, the rest of 2007 was somewhat of a spiritual roller coaster, but there was a definite reduction in the heights and the depths as the year came to an end. The reason I say that is as I review my journal entries, it's clear that my life was coming together, but there were a few low moments or days still to come before life seemed to get back on track.

Chapter Twenty-Two
On The Mend

In December of 2007, I made a quick trip back to La Union to confess and apologize to my closest friends there for my moral failures. They received my confession and offered forgiveness. How wonderful it felt to receive Christ-like forgiveness for the first time in this episode. They promised to pray for me and I promised to return when God allowed.

I continued counseling, both on my own and with Dina. My counselor had asked me to investigate sex addiction twelve-step programs in September and I did. That was very much an eye-opening experience. Although I never believed that I was a sex addict, I went to several programs because it was part of the counseling process. My visits to the first few groups convinced me that sex addiction was not my problem. I didn't say much at the meetings, but did a lot of listening.

After hearing most of the testimonies about the struggles with pornography and adulterous encounters, I felt like a boy scout. But after a few meetings, I was able to see that an addiction to sex was not my problem. A short time later a gentleman named Gary, called me at the request of one of my counselors and invited me to attend a Christian twelve-step program that was for all sorts of struggles, not just sex-related issues. It was that program that started me on a path that God would use to put my life back together.

The program is called *Celebrate Recovery*. I wasn't very familiar with twelve step programs in general, and *Celebrate Recovery* was also twelve-step based, but this program was a study of the twelve-steps from a biblical perspective. At the end of my first visit, I knew that this study was going to help me. Now I'm probably going to sound naive, but I'd never been in any kind of group therapy before, so the open group discussions that were part of

Celebrate Recovery were like a breath of fresh air to me. Once again, I didn't say much at first, I just listened. The freedom that these men felt in sharing their struggles was amazing to me.

This program was not just for sex addicts, although there were several there. The meeting was a group of approximately twelve men who struggled with all kinds of habits and addictions, such as alcohol, drugs, and sex. There were also men there who referred to general struggles that they called "life issues." I could immediately identify with several of the struggles I heard, and I began to connect with several of the guys. Another thing that got my attention, was that all these men with these huge struggles, were professing and many practicing Christians. I'd been around church long enough to know that there is a great fear of confessing sins in church because of the risk of being judged and chastised. It was extremely refreshing to be able to share feelings with brothers about common struggles candidly.

Soon after I began going to *Celebrate Recovery*, I also began trying to meet with several of the guys one-on-one. The first guy I met with, didn't go that well, but he did share some experiences and his story was hard to digest, to say the least. He had been a missionary in Europe and began to struggle with pornography and eventually same-sex attraction. He too decided to confess his struggles to his administrative authority and their response as he told it was shocking to me.

They told him that more than half the missionaries on their staff struggled with pornography. He never told me the mission organization he was with, nor did I ask. He did say that it was one of the well-known organizations, I would recognize their name if he told me. The point is, I don't think it's a secret that today's Church falls short of being the spiritual force God desires it to be in the Bible. But if it's true that the Church's primary group of evangelists are struggling in the way this man testified to, how can we expect anything different.

As I got deeper into the twelve-step study program and began additional reading, I read studies that report that as many as 70% of pastors struggle with pornography. I don't know how many of these reports are accurate, but if there is any truth in them at all, is it any wonder that the church is so weak?

The next guy I connected with was Marc. We hit it off right away and he continues to be one of my best friends today. As our relationship developed and our trust for one another grew, we were able to share our deepest darkest secrets. It's amazing how freeing it can be to get things on the table and when you find that you are not the only one, that there are others struggling with the same things you are. Not only can you share how you are dealing with issues, you can pray for each other in a specific way that releases the power of God in our battles.

I believe that these types of relationships are exactly what God has in mind for his children. Gary, the fellow that invited me to the *Celebrate Recovery* group became a good friend as well. I made several other friends in the group, but Marc and Gary were the ones that I felt closest to and who helped me the most. With the combination of my relationship with God growing increasingly stronger, and those guys cheering me on, by January of 2008, I began to feel like I was walking on solid ground again. But there was going to be another sign that God would provide to assure me that I was on the right track.

When I closed out my financial year and was preparing my taxes, I realized that I had only paid off about $700 of the principal on my debt. I had worked my butt off and paid over $6,000 per month in payments, but because of the interest, I had only paid off $700 of a $250,000 mountain of debt. That was depressing, to say the least. As I prayed and complained to God and was feeling sorry for myself, an amazing thing happened. God said, "Quit your job." My response was, "If I can't pay off my debt with a six-figure income, how can I pay it off with no income?" Again, I heard it. "Quit your job!"

It was such a clear and undeniable message from God that I had to formulate a plan to be obedient. I bargained with God to give me a month to get my affairs in order and I proceeded to do so. First, I had to take care of some health issues. I had an excellent health care program where I was working, so I decided to get a complete physical before I quit. I knew I would have one problem for sure. In 2001 while I was self-employed, I was making a project inspection and fell off a ten-foot ladder, landing on my right shoulder. At the time, we had had a flurry of workers' compensation claims by our employees, so in fear of getting our insurance premiums raised, I decided not to go to the doctor. My shoulder was so bad, that I'd lost almost all strength in that arm and I couldn't raise it above my head. But I learned to live with it. But now, I'd could see what it would take to fix it.

The rest of the physical went well, but when I had my shoulder looked at, the doctor told me what I already knew that I'd lost almost all the strength in my right arm. The doctor scheduled me for a cat scan and told me he would call me with the results. Two weeks went by and I didn't hear anything. I was nearing the end of the 30 days that I'd asked the Lord for, so I called the doctor. It was Thursday, the doctor's day off, so I spoke to one of his assistants. She looked at my file and said she didn't see anything to worry about. I thought that was strange because I knew my shoulder still hurt terribly. But she assured me that if something were wrong the doctor would have called me.

I went to work the next morning with the intention of giving my 30-day notice. I figured that would give God a month to show me what was next. But my bosses were so mad that I planned to leave, they told me to pack my things and get out immediately. No thirty-day notice, no severance pays, and it would soon get worse.

On Saturday morning I got a call from my doctor. He apologized for not getting back to me and told me that I had a serious tear in my rotator cuff along with a major bone spur. He was amazed and wondered how I could walk around without pain meds. He went on to tell me that I needed surgery and after surgery, I would have to immobilize my arm for six weeks. I told him I was no longer employed and had neither the money nor the time for the surgery. All I could think was, *God, what have you done to me?*

Chapter Twenty-Three
On The Road to Recovery

I went to church the next morning praying for anything to give me direction. As the church service began, one of the pastors asked if there was anyone who needed prayer for a physical ailment. I was at the front of the church like a shot. One of the elders prayed for me and instantly, my shoulder felt better. It wasn't perfect, but it was probably ninety percent better. The pastor then said, "you might not get one hundred percent healing this morning, but it's coming." At the same time the healing was taking place, I sensed the Holy Spirit say, "I'm healing you because of your obedience in quitting your job."

The next morning, when I got up and my shoulder was perfect. I continued to pray for direction and once again felt that I received a clear answer from the Lord. He gave me three simple objectives. "Continue to seek me with all your heart, get out of debt and finish the mission base that was started in La Union." That first objective was easy, getting closer to God had already become my priority. And getting out of debt, sounded great, but I still didn't know how that was going to happen.

The mission base in La Union was something that had been evolving in my mind quite awhile. I always felt it was God-inspired, but I can't really remember when the idea first started to take root. While we had the bilingual school, I had bought a small house next to the church we had built and started improving it. Somewhere along the way, it began being called The Mission Base.

The concept was that most American Christians never go on a mission trip because they are afraid of the food or the water or the living conditions on the mission field. If we were to build a facility that addressed those fears, people could come and still have the basic comforts of the U.S. but be able to walk out the front door and be on a third-world mission field. It was a great concept, but it would take a considerable amount of money to complete. I knew that God has lots of money, he just needed to show me how and when He was going to make the transfer.

So, although the three objectives were clear, I was still waiting for God's plan for eliminating the debt and the completion of the mission base. God never gave me a plan like I wanted, but He did it in a way that was better than that, the phone started ringing. I got a call from an old customer who told me he had a perfect project for me. I told him I didn't have a company anymore. Undeterred, he told me to set one up and come and pick up some drawings for pricing a bid on a new project. Within a week, I had established a new company and had a purchase order for approximately $400,000 of work.

I didn't have a shop anymore, so I contacted a friend who had at one time been a competitor and asked if he would be interested in fabricating the project for me. He said yes. Now all I needed was some credit to buy the materials. For the previous fourteen months, I'd been paying all my old suppliers as I'd agreed. So, they were more than happy to reopen my accounts and extend me credit because this would further expedite my payments to them.

I was back in business. Within a few months, I received a call from another old customer who gave me another purchase order, this one for $500,000. We really began to roll.

I continued going to counseling with Dina, but we really weren't getting anywhere. We even were dating occasionally, but it was painfully obvious that we were headed in different directions.

On the recovery front, my step study was progressing very well. I was learning a lot about myself and I began to see the common denominators within our group. We had a weekend retreat to work on our 4th step. The fourth step puts you through a process of self-examination where you recall, list, and pray about past experiences that caused hurt, hurt to yourself or hurt you caused others. After that, the next step in the process is to forgive and ask forgiveness.

We scheduled a retreat to work on our 4th step. We went to Gary's ranch in the Texas hill country for a weekend to get away from daily distractions and focus on the task at hand. It was a great time of fellowship, but most of our time was spent alone, working on our personal inventory. I was amazed at how many memories of my childhood and adolescence resurfaced as I did the exercises. I was learning a lot about myself and why I thought and did the things I did. One of the biggest revelations was to realize how I had stuffed so many emotions and hurts down inside me. I was also beginning to learn about codependency. I had begun reading about it and realizing that it was probably my most fundamental problem. I never read any two publications that defined codependency the same way. And there were vast lists of its manifestations. Not being able to find a common definition in all my research, I came up with my own definition that I felt was a composite of all that I'd read. My definition of codependency is *to be an incomplete person, who attempts to complete himself through his relationships with others.*

I knew that was me, but not being able to define a definitive cause, I once again came up with a consensus reason. In my case, codependency seemed to be caused by a childhood that lacked love, at least love that was convincing or love that was demonstrated (I understood it to mean, very little hugging, affection or quality time together with parents). It seems the most commonly recognized cause I found for codependency is not being able to express your feelings. I really identified with that one. Being able to identify these things about me is why I felt the Step 4 exercise helped me so much. I continued the 4th Step process after the retreat and for several more months. One memory led to another, and then another. I thought I'd exhausted my entire inventory of issues, but I later learned the exercise had only loosened some of the old issues, and there was more to come.

It had been years since our last contact, but I received an email from my cousin Joey, and in it, he asked me questions about our childhood. His email triggered an eruption of additional childhood memories, most of them were bad. That started a new flow, and for the next thirty days, my mind was constantly flooded with replaying and reviewing old childhood memories. I think so many memories were coming back was a result of the 4th Step exercises loosening up everything that had been stuffed down so tightly inside me. Night and day there was so much going on in my head that it was hard to accomplish anything else during that time.

It took a month for me to get back to a normal thought pattern. I can't remember ever experiencing anything like what had happened. I was excited about being back in touch with my cousin, but I just couldn't bring myself to be able to respond to his email and write about what I'd been replaying in my mind, primarily my memories of relationships. It was a month before I finally answered his email. I think it bothered Joey that it took me so long to respond, even though he said it didn't.

I continued counseling, the step study and building the new business. I was building a business, but my focus was more on using it to repay debt than building an empire. By late summer I'd begun to put a serious dent in my debt mountain and was even able to make a trip to Honduras to start work on the mission base there.

In early September, Dina filed for divorce, and I was met with mixed feelings. Although I don't think I would have ever initiated a divorce, I wasn't sure how to respond to her filing. I don't think we'd ever become "one flesh" as described in God's Word, but, it was obvious, that we were now farther apart in almost every way than we had ever been. I met with her lawyer and had what I thought was a very good meeting. He was a Christian and I really felt like I was talking with another brother. He told me I had ninety days to respond to the filing.

I prayed and wrestled with my thoughts for two months, then scheduled another meeting with her lawyer. I asked him that if I didn't respond to the filing by the end of November when the filing expired, what would they do? That possibility had apparently been discussed and he answered that Dina had already committed to filing again. So, I decided to agree to it. I told him that in the interest of not spoiling the family's Thanksgiving, I would sign the papers after Thanksgiving weekend. And with very mixed feelings, I did.

It's painful to end a relationship after almost twenty-eight years. I think some of my regrets came from seeing that all the efforts I'd made to stay together despite the pain and suffering had ultimately been in vain. Even when you haven't been getting along, there are many bonds that are formed. Stacie was our biggest bond, and although things weren't the same between Stacie and me, our relationship was improving, and I hoped it would be totally healed someday.

As 2008 was coming to an end, I was becoming stronger and stronger spiritually. As I review some of my journal entries from those days, I could see that God was beginning to give my life a new direction. In a September entry, there is a renewed interest and curiosity about the early or first church as recorded in the second and fourth chapters of Acts. Questions like that seemed to be arising regularly. What did that church really look like? How could the early church be duplicated today? One thought kept coming to me. Dependence on God. The Lord continued to bring this idea to my thoughts. Autumn seemed to bring a flurry of spiritual insights.

Journal Entries from 2008

September 30th

This morning I feel like I had a moment of clarity, I saw faith in Christ in its most fundamental state. Romans 3:27-28 talks about boasting about our faith. God has been showing me, convincing me that I have nothing to offer in my walk with Him except my acknowledgment that I am helpless, worthless and terribly sinful apart from Him, (Matthew 5:3). Considering that acknowledgment, I seek Him as my primary goal in life, (Matthew 6:31-33). He becomes my only hope for life in eternity and kingdom life on this earth. That is fundamental faith. Considering that, I can understand that grounds for boasting are eliminated. I can willingly and enthusiastically throw any eternal crowns at the feet of our Lord and am ready in my earthly walk today to become a conduit of God's love. "We will have the look of love towards others that will convince them that they need to join us in our pursuit of Jesus," (a paraphrased quote from, Practicing His Presence, *by Brother Lawrence, Journal entry, June 1, 1930) People will only join us in our pursuit of God, when they see the love of God in us, and directed at them. I can recall that happening in my encounters with both John Miller and Fran Watts.*

October 4th

I sense God is telling me to pray about, meditate on, and with His guidance establish some priorities. Exciting time, I take that as God telling me He's ready to do something.

October 6th

God continued to reveal the significance and meaning of Spiritual Bankruptcy, (Matthew 5:3), through Oswald Chambers, My Utmost for His Highest. *The most important issue in regeneration is the recognition of the fact by a person that they are sinners and need a savior and that Jesus Christ is their only hope. You can have no hope in your own abilities or talents to navigate life's journey. You can't change the direction or destination of that journey unless Jesus makes it. That concept is the first step to victory. I now consider the understanding of Matthew 5:3 as the threshold of Kingdom Thinking. All scripture and correct spiritual perspective revolve around that foundation issue.* We can only claim the rest of God's promises with that truth understood as a given. And only then we can begin to step out in victory on the rest of God's promises as he directs us through His Spirit. *That sounds fundamental and it is, but saying you believe it and living it out are two totally different things.*

October 10th

When the answer to every question in my life is Jesus, I'm on the right track.

October 13th

Today Oswald Chambers shed light, (pardon the pun) on the familiar word "Incandescent." It is the light that is generated by a substance being heated or by current passing through it. Light that is totally dependent on its source to be light.

In late 2008, during one of my visits to Honduras, I was sitting on the back porch of the house where I was staying. As I drank my coffee, I noticed the girl working next door, doing laundry by hand. It was about 5:00 AM and still dark, so I could only see her silhouette, but I noticed how hard she was working as the sun was coming up beyond her. I thought to myself, I need someone who works as hard as she does to take care of the mission base. I watched her for several more days and decided to approach her. I asked her if she was happy working there and she said no. I told her that I was looking for someone to start living at the mission base in February and taking care of it. She was interested and without much more discussion, I hired her. Her name was Adela.

By year's end, I had paid off most of my debt and the mission base was almost ready to move into. At that point, I felt like I was walking in the clouds. I had started the year at probably the lowest spiritual point of my life and I was finishing with almost a totally new life. Is God amazing or what?

When I prepared my tax return in March of 2009, I found that in addition to being out of debt, I was now operating considerably in the black. I had been making monthly trips to Honduras and projected that the mission base would be completed enough to move into by June. I was experiencing Recovery!

At this point, I need to do a little reflecting. Reflecting on where I'd been and where I was. In January of 2007, I felt I could go no lower and had little hope of ever doing more than just paying off the past. By the end of the year, I'd sunk even lower, and I felt there was no hope of ever being anything other than the earth's refuse. Then, in January of 2008, I recall making the statement to God, "If anything ever comes of me in the future, if I'm to be anything but the scum of the earth, it will have to be by Your hand." It was about that time that God told me to quit my job and things began to turn around. That is a reinforcement of my insights about Matthew 5:3.

Now at the end of 2008, I felt I'd been totally restored spiritually and financially. I was once again walking in the confidence of a clean and pure heart, knowing God was with me in all that I did. Not only did I feel that He was with me, but that He was the one directing me and orchestrating the events of my life. Through the *Celebrate Recovery* step study and through other studying that it had inspired, I had come to a place where I understood my past or at least why I had such problems with life and why I had problems with relationships, boundaries, authority, and morality. *There's a lot of freedom in knowing who we are and why we do things because we can begin to recognize approaching situations and take proper precautions not to make the same disastrous mistakes that had plagued the past.*

As I reflected on all the hurt my past actions had caused to others and myself, there was one question that I couldn't get past. That was, why did God wait until I was sixty years old to reveal all this to me?

Chapter Twenty-Four
Back to Normal????

2009 was a year of building on the foundation that God had re-established in my life, the spiritual foundation of my relationship with God through Jesus Christ, and a sound financial foundation, where I didn't owe anything but a truck payment which I could have paid off if I wanted to. Finally, I had a direction. The mission base in La Union was almost habitable and although, I wasn't sure how it would operate, I was sure that its operation was the direction God was taking me.

I titled this chapter "Back To Normal????" with question marks because I don't think there really is such a thing as normal, at least in life's journey as a Christian. One of the biggest conflicts we have as believers, in my opinion, is that we try to make God and His plans fit into what we think should be normal. It's unfortunate, but I think that concept is what keeps us from being supernatural players in God's kingdom plan.

As I re-read my journal, I see that the year seemed to start with God reinforcing four primary spiritual concepts:

1) Continuing to embrace spiritual bankruptcy
2) Confirming forgiveness and God's desire for reconciliation,
3) Attitude of surrender.
4) Attitude of total dependence.

Journal entries from 2009

January 16

Luke 15:31" My son, you are always with me and everything I have is yours." When we come to that realization, I believe we have crossed the threshold and entered the kingdom of God

January 20

I realize my availability is all I have to offer God.

January 22

John 12:24 "Unless a kernel of wheat falls to the ground and dies, it remains a single seed." I've come to realize that it's all about dying and receiving. We come to the point of desperation in each area of our life as we grow. Until we encounter and understand our hopelessness and spiritual bankruptcy, we cannot receive God's life in that area of our life. We cannot receive God's life until we have no life of our own.

January 23

Joshua 1:5 "I will never leave you nor forsake you." I'm realizing that God's promise to Israel and His promise to us at salvation is more permanent and powerful than any sin we can commit.

March 5

John 1:12, a verse that has always grabbed me. "He gave the right to become children of God." As I read Agape Road, the author points out on Page 244 that Just as an acorn has all the potential of becoming a giant oak tree, as believers, we have all the potential of becoming a child of God. God waits and wants that to happen. If the acorn gets in the proper environment, rich moist soil, nothing can stop it from becoming a giant oak. If we totally submit/yield to God, the same is true for us. I used to teach that concept only using an apple seed.

April 9

I'm writing because I haven't in a while. I've come to the end of the journey that the Lord sent me on at the beginning of 2008. I feel like I'm back to having a solid relationship with God, I'm out of debt and the mission base is complete lacking just a little finish work. What now? I plan to fast from TV this week and spend the weekend seeking the Lord.

April 15

I've concluded that God is now removing all signs of direction to draw me to a position of total dependence before we move forward. Every potential project and all progress in plan development except for my day to day work has stopped.... I feel like I'm about to learn what unbroken abiding is about... What an exciting time!

April 26

In response to questions about the mission base today, twice, I made the statement that I'm not a missionary. The second time I said it, I felt that maybe I've been clinging too tightly to the Celebrate Recovery program when God is trying to get me to move on. I can't help but ask the question, am I hiding in the recovery process/program?

May 5

Gary gave me a workbook entitled, "Conquering Codependency." Another Twelve-Step study, only this is exclusively from a codependency standpoint. As I finished the first step, I feel I must proclaim one of those milestone moments of realization. Since starting the step studies in 2008, I've gradually realized that codependency is the root issue in all my shortcomings in life. Today I've been able to connect a lot of dots in the whys of my life, both before and after becoming a Christian. I see that my codependency, (my need for approval, need to be needed and compulsion to rescue or fix others) has caused me to enter ministries that are more about medicating me than serving others. I've never been able to complete a cycle of ministry; each ministry venture always seems to unravel before it's complete. I've heard more than one sermon dealing with the issue that, "a need does not always constitute a call." I think I've seen needs of others as opportunities to medicate myself. Several months ago, I began to realize the reality of Romans 7:18, "that there is no good in me" which opened my spiritual eyes to Matthew 5:3, "blessed are the poor in spirit," which confirms that we are totally dependent on God to live this Christian life effectively... Therefore, we must abide constantly (John 15:5) in God, (be constantly connected), to see, recognize, evaluate (our motivations) and respond to ministry opportunities.

May 16

Step three in Conquering Codependency *has introduced me to the term double binding. It's when we make impossible goals for ourselves, then get depressed when we can't achieve them. The story of my life.*

The *Conquering Codependency* step study really helped me put a lot of the pieces together. It is biblically based as is *Celebrate Recovery*, so it fits very well with the rest of my recovery efforts. For several months I focused on that study and putting the finishing touches on the mission base. Adela had moved into the mission base in April and started taking care of the place. It was obvious right away that Adela and I connected. But she is nearly forty years younger than me, so I knew it would never go anywhere.

In May I hired Magdelena, a second girl to help Adela and live at the mission base. She is Adela's cousin and is close to the same age. Adela didn't really need help, but I thought it would be wise for someone to be living in the house with Adela and me when I was there and someone to live with Adela when I wasn't.

Living there, even part-time took some getting used to. The living conditions and the culture were major adjustments for me. I was living about ten days a month there and although our living conditions were far better than our neighbors, they were a long way from what I was used to.

June 10

Last night I took my first hot shower in the La Union mission base. It has been such a struggle to get to this point. We still have leaks and lots to do, but we are functional. I need to begin to settle in now and take life as God gives it to me. I must rest in his joy.

As time went on, we adjusted at the mission base to make it more functional and more comfortable, and it began to feel more and more like home. Maybe because it was becoming home. Adela and I continued to grow closer, but I continued to say, "there's no way a relationship can become permanently successful when there's a difference in age like ours."

August 11

I finally feel like I'm settling in in La Union. I'm going to bed early and getting up early, I read before bed last night and had a two and one-half hour quiet time this morning. My relationship with Adela is hitting a good stride spiritually. I feel like I'm being called to a new level of total dependency on God.

September 1

As I prepare to return to Houston, I feel like I'm leaving home... I feel my heart is now connected here.... This is now my home. I don't think it will be long before I'll be living here full time.

As I've had the opportunity to move back and forth between here and Houston so frequently, I can't help but notice that the quality of life here is far better than in the states. They have fewer "things and comforts" but relational living is much better. People have time and use every opportunity to visit with family, neighbors and friends. As people pass each other on the street, they always say hello, and usually stop to visit. People take naps here, it used to make me crazy, I felt they were wasting time sleeping, but now I've come to think that if you can nap, why not. I've only lived here a short time, but I know nearly everyone on my street, back in Houston in the last house we owned, I knew very few of my neighbors.

While the slower pace of La Union offers an opportunity for a better quality of life and time to develop more intimate personal relationships, that freedom combined with a very backward morality has taken a toll on the family structure and the character of the town. As 2009 was coming to an end, I began to sense some things in La Union that had not been obvious before. I began to sense evil. I'd known all along that La Union was a moral cesspool. Very few normal families, that is with a husband and wife living together with their children. Many of the men have several regular sex partners or so-called "wives." Usually, the number of wives a man has is dictated by how many women he could afford to house. Most girls have already had a baby by the time they are eighteen. I've read statistics that eighty percent of Honduran girls have had a baby by age eighteen. I'd known about those kinds of things all along, but I was beginning to sense a presence of evil.

October 1

I'm sensing an awareness of evil in La Union. I sense a call to focus on my spiritual health. I also sense that moving here will not be a retirement picnic, but a spiritual war.

At the other end of the scale, I was beginning to grasp a little better, the depths of God's love.

October 11

One thing, probably the biggest thing I've learned on this journey, is the vastness of God's love. Or maybe I should say I've begun to experience or embrace God's love.... The verse "I love because He first loved me, (1 John 4:19)." I don't think we can appreciate God's love until we begin to learn the depths of our sinfulness.

November 11

Another milestone in sight, the biggest obstacle or struggle during recovery is being able to forgive me for my adulterous, sinful actions. I think in years past, self-forgiveness for sins wasn't so hard because I was living a life of good works that I was impressed with. Maybe I thought I was worthy of forgiveness. But now, all that so-called worthiness is gone. Truth is, I was never worthy of God's forgiveness or love. I think that's why His love seems so special now. He's more interested in my surrender than my works.

November 17

Oswald Chambers wrote in today's devotional, the promises of God don't come to life until we understand and the nature of God. When God speaks, He speaks to His own nature within us.

I've reached the point of understanding what it means to want nothing but God. Not what He has, but only Him. I'm ready to move to Honduras and be whatever God wants me to be.

In mid-December, I shared with Adela that I felt God was calling me to move to Honduras and that we should talk seriously about our future together. I tried to the best of my ability to share all the negative possibilities that lie ahead in a marriage with a forty-year age differential, but also shared how deep my love for her was. I told her that considering all the negative possibilities, if she still wanted to marry me, I would be honored to have her as my wife. She immediately said, "yes." Over the next few weeks, we set the dates for my move to Honduras and our marriage. The 12th and 15th of January. I returned to Houston on December 29th to prepare for the move.

Chapter Twenty-Five
New Year, New Country, New Chapter, New Life

I spent New Year's Day 2010 and the next ten days packing, moving and all that goes along with moving to another country. I had accumulated a fair amount of furniture and housewares that I wasn't sure I wanted to get rid of, so I made a deal with my friend Dino who had just moved into a house with no furniture. The deal was that he could use my furniture, if I could store my boxed-up housewares there and have a rent-free room for my visits to Houston. It was a good deal for both of us. I also took one last physical to make sure everything was in working order.

I was prepared to leave on January 12th, but the night before, my doctor's assistant called me and told me that I was seriously anemic. This was something new and it was apparently so bad that she made me promise that I would see a doctor about it as soon as I got to Honduras. One of the reasons that I had scheduled the physical was because I was feeling so run down while I was moving. I had to stop and catch my breath every few minutes. Thank God I did have the physical before leaving the U.S.

I left on the twelfth and found an English-speaking doctor as soon as I got to Honduras. I told him of my wedding and honeymoon in two days, so he gave me some iron supplements and scheduled me for additional tests after the honeymoon.

We had a simple wedding at a hotel in San Pedro Sula, one of the two largest cities in Honduras. Adela's family came along with a few friends. We had a total of about twenty-six guests. Even though we were two hours late getting started because the witnesses were late, it was a very nice wedding. My friend Victor officiated, his daughter Rebecca sang, and Adela and I were married. This wasn't my first marriage, but this was the first one that I was excited about. Adela was and is an amazing young lady and even though there is forty years difference in our ages, we seemed to complement each other in a supernatural way. As Rocky Balboa so profoundly stated in the movie, *Rocky*: "She's got gaps, I've got gaps, but together we got no gaps."

We went to the island of Roatan for our honeymoon and had a great time. When we returned to La Union I was rested and ready to find out what was happening with my blood. It was the doctor's opinion that I must be losing blood somewhere internally, but after $1500 dollars' worth of testing (probably equivalent to $15,000 dollars for the same tests in the US), they found nothing. So, we continued on iron supplements and that seemed to get me by, at least for a while.

For most of 2010, I spent time working in the garden at the mission base. And there was a lot of work to do. The mission base was livable, but still needed a lot of tweaking to make it as comfortable as I had hoped. I'd never been big on creature comforts and anything we did was an upgrade compared to what Adela was used to. She had grown up in a small settlement with a dirt floor and no electricity, so this was mostly new for her. But I don't really think she was that worried about comfort, she was just happy to be my wife. I don't remember ever feeling as loved as Adela made me feel. I felt like she was living to make me happy.

I can't remember loving anyone in the same way I love her. I felt like she was really part of me. I remember her telling me some time back, that I was the only person that she has ever trusted completely. I think that's the way we're supposed to feel in a Christian marriage. This may sound silly or stupid or probably selfish, but it was the first time in my life that I wanted to give someone else the best plate of food. For example, I love ribeye steak, especially when it looks like a perfect cut. I don't ever remember wanting to give the best steak to someone else, but that was how I began to think. For that matter, I still do. We were partners, it was and is an amazing feeling. Once again, I think we were and are experiencing what God had in mind for His children's marriages.

In years past, I remember being totally impressed by my daughter Stacie's marriage to Mitch. I witnessed several of their arguments while visiting them and several seemed serious to the point where as a father, I had some brief concerns about their marriage. But then I realized that even though the argument seemed bitter, when it was over, it was over. At the writing of this chapter, Adela and I have been married eight years. And we can argue with the best of them, but when it's over, it's over and there's no carry over into the next argument. Neither of us gets "historical" as they say. There's no bringing up the past. I think that's one of the major things that makes our marriage special.

Not to be judgmental, but in hindsight and sixty plus years' experience, I think a lot of people, Christian people rush into marriage driven by their emotions, hormones, and pressures rather than seeking God's wisdom. If God truly does have a plan for our lives, which I'm convinced that He does, that means He has a mate for us as well. My advice for young Christian couples is to pray until you have a peace that the person you are intending to wed is the person that God planned for you to wed.

Chapter Twenty-Six
Ministry Takes a Turn

Adela and I continued to piddle, putter and tweak without too much thought about being a mission base. Although God had inspired an urgency in getting the base constructed and ready for guests, we felt that He would be the promoter, so we didn't really put much effort into promoting its opening. Life had taken a major turn and slowed down considerably for both of us. For now, we were enjoying our new marriage and the new freedom in our schedules. We both spent more time each day with God, but other than that we were both so caught up in our new marriage that we didn't think about much else. We spent a lot of time working in the garden and enjoying our periods of rest laying together on our new garden hammock. Often, after we finished our day's work, we would lay there and watch the sunset. Life was good, good.

One challenge that God gave me early on was our neighbor across the street. Her name was Lola and she was a tough woman. During the early days in the construction of the mission base, she used to regularly shout at me in the street to go home, that I wasn't wanted here. God's challenge was that if I could win Lola over for the kingdom, we could reach anyone. God used Lola in one of my first serious lessons in dependence on God. The lesson was, that only God knows what needs to be said or done in a person's life to bring them to salvation. It doesn't matter how good my intentions are or how strong my love for them if I'm not taking my direction from God who knows all things, in my every effort to win Lola to the Kingdom, my efforts will probably be fruitless. Sure enough, God was faithful to that mandate. During the next several months, He would prompt me in my every thought, word and action towards Lola.

Even though we had not done much promotion of the mission base, once again God was faithful and people began to come. We had three groups visit in 2010. Our first visitors were the Cox family. If you remember, Robert was my first friend at Encourager Church. He and his wife Kristin and their boys, Cooper, Keller, and Kade came in April and helped with some painting. I think they came primarily to encourage us, which they did, and we really enjoyed their visit. Later that year, we also had a visit from Houston's *Encourager Church* youth ministers, Rich and Tracy Nickel. They came back several times after that with groups of kids from the church. We also housed a group that was constructing a church in one of the nearby settlements. So, went our first year. As I write this, it doesn't seem like we did much, but it occupied all our time.

As we neared the end of the year Adela made a comment that would once again change our direction. Being a local herself, she pointed out that although she loved our life as a mission base hosts our house was empty most of the time. I agreed and added that I was fine with that. She continued to say that there were a lot of children in the settlements that couldn't complete their high school education because they have no place or means to live here in La Union where the junior and senior high schools are located.

Let me clarify. La Union is the principal city of a municipality that encompasses approximately forty-eight settlements and villages. Most of them have elementary schools that go up to sixth grade, but if students want to continue their education and complete high school, they must come to school in La Union. Because of the distances and road conditions, it's not possible to make a daily trip from a settlement into town and back for school. Most of the families in the settlements are too poor to pay for their children to be housed and fed here, so unless they have family here to stay with, most children from the settlements never get more than a sixth-grade education.

Adela continued by asking if we might help some of the settlement kids by giving them a place to stay. I really didn't want to do it. I told her that I had already raised my own kids and really didn't want to raise anyone else's. As we talked more I learned that she had some specific students in mind, her sister Edita and her niece Sindy. Edita, who was sixteen had finished sixth-grade four years earlier but had no way to continue her education. Sindy and her cousin Estela, who we also agreed to let stay with us, were only nine-years-old, but lived too far from the settlement school to attend there regularly. Sindy was still in first-grade, and Estela had advanced to third grade. God touched my heart, and I reluctantly agreed to let Edita, Sindy, and Estela come and live with us to start attending school in La Union in January of 2011.

Edita was a very quiet girl who rarely said anything. She was reluctant to speak even when asked a question, but with time, she gradually changed. I can see now that she was one of those humble ones who was growing beneath the surface, then suddenly she began to blossom. She went on to do very well in school.

I don't think Sindy really wanted to go to school. She didn't do very well and only stayed with us one year.

Within a few days of registering Estela, the school let us know that although her papers said she was in the third-grade, she was far behind, and they felt she should be in the first-grade. They gave her ninety days to catch up or she would be placed back in the first-grade.

As soon as I agreed to let the girls stay with us, I ran an employment ad in the newspaper looking for someone to serve as a governess and tutor. Several applied, and we decided on a young university student who was taking a year off from her studies. She offered to work as a volunteer. She said she felt that God was telling her to offer and after several interviews, we accepted her offer. Her name was Jessy and seemed to fit in very well right away. She was a serious girl and she spoke reasonably good English, so she also began helping me as a translator.

Jessy immediately connected with Estela and together, they not only got Estela on the level, but Estela went on to finish the year at the top of her class. Jessy played a big part in that, but it was primarily Estela's desire that made it happen. Everyone was so impressed with Estela's achievements that she was given an opportunity to take a scholarship acceptance test at a Christian bilingual school, also located in La Union. She did well on the test and was given a scholarship for the fourth grade.

The La Union public school calendar is scheduled around the coffee harvest. Everything revolves around coffee. Everyone either grows coffee, picks coffee or works in a coffee processing facility. The coffee harvest begins in November and ends in February, so the public schools start their school year in February and end in November. On the other hand, the bilingual school schedule is the same as the U.S. school schedule, August through June.

Word got out that we were allowing students to stay with us, so in August of 2011 we were contacted by the bilingual school leadership and asked if we would take in some of their students. They had given scholarship tests in some of the settlements and had five students to whom they were willing to give scholarships, but they would need a place to stay. I really don't remember how they convinced me, but they did. So, by August, we had eight students living with us. If it sounds like I was very much opposed to the whole idea of keeping kids, I was. My reluctance was based on my opinions of the typical American high school students I knew. I felt that all they seemed to care about is television and video games and that they seemed to walk around with attitudes of entitlement most of the time.

It didn't take long to realize that these kids were different. Most of them had a sincere desire to learn and they were very obedient. As I was around them more, my attitude began changing.

As of the writing of this book, Estela is now sixteen, an honor student in the tenth grade and is our primary translator in our house. Edita, now twenty-three, quietly continued her education and graduated high school with honors. She is now a second-year law student and has grown to be one of our strongest leaders. She took over as the director of our Oansa/Awana program, as well as becoming a leader in several other capacities within our ministry, but I'm getting ahead of myself.

As our new student housing ministry continued, God began to make modifications to the program. He was clearly moving us in the direction of being a ministry of hope to our youth. Instead of just being a ministry that supplied food and housing to underprivileged children while trying to model Christian values, we began to take on the characteristics of a discipleship ministry. We started having a family devotion one night a week. It was like a family meeting where we discussed family business, but we also started discussing, learning and memorizing one Bible verse each week. One of the students asked if he could sing a Christian song during the devotion, which became a weekly event.

By the end of the first school year, our family meeting had become a time of worship and discipleship. God also led me to regularly state the concept that God had created everyone with a specific plan for their lives, (Psalm 139:15-16). As time went on, that concept was becoming the theme and foundation purpose of our ministry.

While we couldn't make a student become a Christian, everyone was required to live according to the house rules which were biblically based. And we continued to stress the concept that God has a plan for our life that is the most fulfilling path that our life can possibly take, and that plan couldn't be fully embraced and realized unless we establish an intimate relationship with God through Jesus Christ. After ten years of trying on my own to establish programs and projects that would give hope to the youth of La Union, God had made it happen. We were a ministry of hope to the youth of La Union.

As the student ministry progressed, we began to see how we were affecting the people in the neighborhood. The family grocery store across the street was flourishing because of our business. But beyond the economic impact, we were seeing spiritual encouragement as well. We started holding worship services in some of the settlements that our kids were from. We were also getting reports from the school teachers about what a positive influence our students were having on the other students.

And there was the Lola project. I tried to be nice in my own way to Lola, but God was prompting me as well in my ministry to her. Once when I was in San Pedro Sula, I felt God prompting me to buy a package of fresh strawberries for Lola. There were never any fresh strawberries in La Union unless someone brought them from a faraway town like San Pedro Sula. Lola was genuinely touched by the gesture. She said, "I'm sorry, but I don't have money to pay for these." I said, "They're a gift." Another time when I was in Santa Barbara, I felt God prompt me to buy a small roasted chicken for her. Once again, she was obviously touched.

She stopped yelling at me, but I still wasn't sure I was making any progress in my relationship with her until one day there was a plumbing problem. Our house wastewater line ran under her yard to the main sewage canal. Our line had collapsed, was backing up and needed to be replaced. She refused to let us service the portion of the line that was under her yard. She said her deal for the easement was with the previous property owner and not with me. I tried to explain that the easement went with the house, not the owner, but she refused to give in. I even offered to pay her, she was not a wealthy woman, she was rather poor. I didn't lose my temper because once again, I felt God was prompting me that she was one of my primary ministries, so I just prayed.

The next day Lola came over and told me we could dig up her yard to replace the line. And she wasn't going to charge me. Wow! That event broke the ice and we became friends. She began coming over occasionally for lunch and about a year later she went with us to the Baptist church next door for Easter service. She continued to go to that church and she became a Christian. Although we have our ups and downs, Lola and I remain friends.

In January of 2012, we added a few more students and we began to struggle financially. I had not planned to be a missionary that required outside support when I moved to Honduras, so I had no financial support network. Adela and I had been doing fine on my retirement income, and we even did okay when we only had a few students, but feeding, housing and clothing thirteen were more than a little different. It was considerably more expensive. We went through our cash reserves and started accumulating balances on our credit cards. I didn't know what to do. We had become so attached to the kids that I didn't even consider sending them home. Then in December of that year, I had to have an emergency gallbladder and hernia surgery, which pushed us over the financial edge. We had been living under financial stress for about six months. We were struggling with every decision to spend money. We didn't buy anything we didn't absolutely have to, but we were getting deeper and deeper into debt, then something happened.

I was in San Pedro Sula in late December buying our supplies when I saw a bag of Christmas candy in the grocery store. It wasn't even a big bag, and it only cost five dollars. I thought to myself, wouldn't the kids enjoy this. But I just couldn't justify spending the five dollars. I thought and prayed about that during the entire three-hour drive home. I prayed,

> *"Father, I don't believe you want us to live like this. You promise us in Matthew 6:31-33, that if we seek you and your kingdom righteous first, it's your responsibility to take care of our needs. From now on, we will continue to be frugal, but we're not going to live thinking that you will punish us if we step off this financial tightrope."*

God made another thing clear to me as 2012 ended. I had made my living in the steel business by specializing in difficult projects, projects that no one else wanted or were afraid to do. Projects with a difficult schedule, difficult design, difficult location or any combination of those things. To make a profit, I would have to get very creative. I had become so successful in doing those type projects that I had become a little arrogant concerning my creative abilities. That self-confidence carried over into my life as a Christian.

I always said I was trusting God, but, I was trusting more in my creativity, tenacity and hard work than I was on God. I think the primary purpose why God had brought me to the end of myself was to make that point. I remember clearly one time during that period while in meditation or prayer, God made it clear to me that no matter how intelligent I thought I was, how creative or hard-working, *if I expected to be successful as a missionary in Honduras, it was only going to happen if I maintained an intimate relationship with Him. I had to learn to hear the voice of His Spirit and be obedient to His direction, immediately and completely.*

From that point, I felt that things were going to start to turn around. And they did. In early 2013, I had a call from my friend Joe from Celebrate Recovery. He and my friend Marc wanted to come and visit and help with some needed maintenance. Joe later came again with another group, and because of that, still others came and after that, we also began receiving donations, some of them from people we didn't even know. It wasn't that our finances had instantly turned around, but it was obvious that God was doing things to supplement our efforts. Before 2013 was over, several Christian businessmen from Houston began visiting and making donations by providing ministry shirts and brochures which was also a big encouragement.

Understand, that when I moved to Honduras, it was to retire. There was no support network or plan other than God's for any of what we were now doing. I still didn't speak Spanish and was totally dependent on translators of which Adela was primary. And as hard as she tried, her English was not that good.

The ministry was evolving solely under God's hand as He presented and allowed events to take place. In 2014, the men who had begun visiting in 2013 set out to establish a 501c3 nonprofit corporation for us so that it would be easier to get donations. As the public school started the new school year, we were up to 26 students, which continued to stretch us financially. But in the spring, I had an opportunity to do consulting work in Houston for a friend who was a steel fabricator and someone I'd worked with in the past. Adela and I considered it an answer to prayer, so I began to start spending one week per month in Houston. It was a little tough on Adela for me to be gone, but she knew we needed the money so she tried not to complain.

Adela did a great job dealing with the daily issues of 26 students living under one roof, but things were starting to get a little more complicated. Some of the students had become Christians and it was obvious that some of them were still lost. Everyone was trying to at least appear to be following the rules, even though some of their hearts were not in it. Painfully, we had to send some students home for not being able to adjust to life in the house, but our core of believers was growing.

In May we started an *OANSA* program focusing on the local children ages seven through fourteen. *OANSA* is the Central American version of the American *AWANA* program. It mixes Bible verse and concept memory with games. We meet for an hour and a half each week and the kids love it. Our program starts at 3:30 pm on Sundays and the kids usually start gathering at 2:30 waiting to get in. We used our older students as leaders and honestly, we really struggled through our first year. Fortunately, one of the local bilingual teachers, Nelly, had worked in an *OANSA* program in her hometown and really enjoyed it so she and her husband Miguel helped us and were a big part of getting through that first year. We ministered to approximately one hundred children from the community.

The influence of our ministry was growing. In October our 501c3 application was approved. We entered 2015 starting to look like a professional ministry which seemed good at the time, but I personally began to sense a struggle ahead. Everything seemed to be advancing on all fronts through 2015. Donations were up, and I was being consumed by my steel job. I was managing the steel fabrication for an 18-story parking garage in Houston which was taking more of my time than I had anticipated, but they continued to give me raises so I continued. The board was doing most of the ministry promotion and fundraising, which allowed me to focus on the demands of my project in Houston.

The students were continuing to grow spiritually and were showing some real maturity. They were working together, sharing chores in the house, and we began to study a revised version of *The Colossians 2:7 Series* that had turned my life around back in 1992. Everyone had a full schedule, so we decided, (the kids decided), that we would study the *2:7 Series* at 4:00 AM two mornings a week. That study became a real turning point in the house because it triggered new conversations about having a relationship with God. We began to discuss a lot of ways that a relationship with God effects in our lives.

During the summer one of my old customers invited me to reopen my steel company and do a project for them. I accepted and began to phase myself out of my position managing the parking garage project, which was almost complete. I started gearing up to fabricate the steel for the new steel project, a nine-story medical school building, also in Houston. By year's end, while I still had some serious credit card debt, we began to reach solid ground financially and continued to move in a positive direction.

But the new project turned out to be far more demanding than I had anticipated. The project was advancing at an aggressive pace, and they were making changes at a pace that I could barely keep up with. From September 2015 until February of 2016 it seemed like every spare minute I had was devoted to pricing and implementing those changes. Maybe it was because I'm getting old, and technology is passing me by, but it seemed to be one of the toughest projects I'd ever done.

By February the project had more than doubled in size, but I began to see daylight. As I was able to refocus on more than just the medical building project, there were early warning signs that we were headed into a time of turbulent and very testing waters.

As I look back over my journey as a Christian, I can recall three defining situations that reassure me when trials or doubts arise.

First was the fact that by God's provision, as a business owner, I never missed a payroll. As a small business owner with no line of credit for most of my years in business, I depended almost exclusively on cash flow to meet my obligations. In twenty plus years of meeting a Friday payroll, I never lacked having the money to pay our employees. If you've never been a small business owner with employees, you probably won't understand the miraculous implications of that. What's more, there were many Fridays when I went to work in the morning not knowing how I was going to cover payroll that afternoon. There were a good number of Fridays that I didn't know even at noon how I was going to cover payroll at 3:30. I can't count how many Fridays I received unexpected calls from customers telling me that they had a check for me.

You may ask, isn't that irresponsible? Well, if I was expecting God to supply money we hadn't earned, that would be irresponsible. But sometimes faith does look irresponsible to a non-believer, and maybe to a believer who is not accustomed to walking in faith.

Those experiences proved to me over and over how faithful God is, and how involved He is in all the events and details of our lives.

Another experience that I think about is years ago when one of my customers burned me for $145,000. Basically, they just didn't pay me because they lost money on the project. I had suppliers and employees that I felt I needed to pay regardless whether I got paid or not. I prayed and prayed for wisdom on what to do. I never heard from God but felt that even though I would be in trouble with the IRS, I decided to pay my debts and employees requiring me to use about $30,000 from my tax withholding account. I reported to the IRS what I'd done but didn't get an immediate response as to what action they would take to recover the money.

They kept me waiting for almost six months before they rendered a decision. I had spent everything I had to pay people. I had children in college, and a few other responsibilities, but God chose to allow me to live in a state of limbo for six months. But I clearly remember every morning, God would somehow communicate with me, I could either take a step forward or turn and retreat. There was no turning to the left or right. It was either forward or back. I felt like I was in a long, narrow, deep crevice of stone only as wide as my body. I could not see the end in front of me or behind me. I clung to His promise, "I will never leave you nor forsake you. What are you going to do?" It always seemed obvious to me that I had to daily choose to live that day that God had given me.

I made it through that time, but words can't express what six-months of constantly having to keep my eyes on God has done in teaching me to trust Him.

Finally, years ago, my father and my stepmother died within a few days of each other. They both had been in poor health, but neither was expected to die as soon as they did. One lived in Tennessee and the other in New York. I thought I was not close to either one of them, but something about their deaths affected me deeply. For a week or more, it was like I was in suspended animation. One day I was on my knees praying about it, and I felt a peace that could only be described as God wrapping me in a blanket.

That went on every day for at least a week. It was one of the experiences that changed me forever.

I wish I could say I've grown to the point that my reflexive response to trials is to trust God, but I can't. But if you give me a few minutes, I will usually say, every situation we face is from God or allowed by God and its purpose is either to turn our attention to God, cause us to trust God or to make us more like Christ. 2016 would prove to do all those things and make me realize what my commitment to God and His service really was.

Chapter Twenty-Seven
The Anchor Holds

In February 2016, as I got caught up with my paperwork on the construction project, I began to survey where I was in everything else. I don't want anyone to think that any amount of outside pressure would cause me to compromise my daily responsibilities to my calling in our ministry, but I had gotten to point where there was little visionary or meditation time beyond those daily responsibilities. The students were doing better and better all the time. They were taking over more and more of the ministry responsibilities. They asked to completely take over the running of the *OANSA* ministry. They were holding each other to a higher and higher standard of accountability. And by my biggest indicator of how we're doing in the ministry, the core group of Christian students was continuing to grow in number and in spiritual maturity. The ministry was doing well.

But as my discretionary time began to increase I began to take a closer look at the organizational side of the ministry. I was researching how nonprofit boards operate and was struck to learn that most nonprofit boards are in full control of the assets and the oversight of their designated ministry. I was sure that this was addressing situations where the ministry had been founded, organized, funded and managed by the board from day one. But, because our origins had been from my personal assets, I began to think, this is something that needed to be discussed and clarified.

When I had moved to Honduras I had sold almost all my belongings and invested the money in the development of the mission base which was also now our home. I wanted to make sure that we had an understanding with the board that while I had no problem using the facility, for ministry purposes, I was not willing to surrender control or ownership of my house, the mission base to the board. I tried to convince them that all money raised would be used for ministry costs only and not used for facility improvements or even repairs. I still planned to fund those types of expenses on my own. We were only hoping for financial help in covering the $4,000-$4,500 per month cost to run the ministry.

So, I raised the issue at the next board meeting. I always began and ended each meeting by thanking the board members for their help. I was very sincere in that, I really did appreciate them. After giving them a status report, which was customary, I shared what I'd read about nonprofit boards. I must not have done a very good job because several of them took offense. The discussion from that meeting went on for a few weeks, and it was so strained that three of the original board members resigned. It hurt deeply because I really appreciated all these board members had done. Their presence had helped us move to a new plateau of ministry and helped establish the tax exemption for the ministry to operate under. I think we're all still friends, but in all honesty, their departure was painful for all of us.

Losing the board members was the first major trial of the year, but there were more trials to come. My anemia returned, and it got to the point where I had no energy at all. At one point, I couldn't operate more than a few hours at a time before I had to take a nap. I supposedly found the best hematologist in Honduras and he gave me a transfusion of iron, which helped for about six months. But he warned me that it was not a cure, and we needed to figure out where I was losing blood. I promised to investigate it, but if I was feeling okay, I didn't think much about it.

A short time later, a doctor friend noticed a lesion on my face and told me I needed to get it checked immediately. I had had several bouts with skin cancer since moving to Honduras, because of my carelessness in the sun in my younger years. And I had had several surgeries. I had the lesion checked and sure enough, it needed to be removed. But the doctor, whom I'd gotten to know well, told me that I may have waited too long for this one. I had the surgery and had to take an additional battery of tests to see if it had metastasized. Fortunately, it hadn't. That was a relief.

Things went smoothly for the next month or so until early June. Returning home from a trip to town, I was met by two bandits waiting for me on the road. As I approached them, they motioned with guns drawn for me to stop. Instinct prompted me not to stop, but instead to drive right at them. They began to fire at me. They fired off four or five rounds each before they had to dive out of the way of my oncoming pickup. How they missed me from about twenty feet away had to be by God's protection. After I passed them, they began firing again. They hit the truck a number times, two or three times in the tires, one severing the brake line, one in the tailgate and one in the headache bar right behind my head. I was only three kilometers from the house when it happened, so I was able to get to the tire repair shop before my tires were flat.

They were both wearing bandana masks, but from the expression in their eyes as I approached them, I think I probably scared them more than they scared me, but it was an experience I will never forget. You never know what you'll do in a situation like that until it happens. I thank God that He was in control of my instincts. He was obviously in control of the whole situation. The next few times I went to town, I was a little timid as I passed the spot of that encounter, but after that, I was okay. I came away from the incident thinking that God had shown me that no matter how dangerous the encounter, He was going to protect me.

About a week later I began to feel bad. I'd had a lingering case of what I thought was the flu for about a month with a lot of lung congestion. I was constantly coughing up dark colored phlegm, and now I was beginning to have stomach pains as well. I'm not big on going to the doctor unless I really feel bad. But I got to the point where I couldn't get out of bed except to make regular trips to the toilet to unload from both ends. I finally went to the doctor and found out I was seriously sick. My anemia had flared up again, I had a serious bronchial infection and a colon infection. They put me on IVs for a few hours, gave me some medication, chewed me out for waiting too long to come to the doctor then finally let me go home.

After nearly a week in bed, I started feeling better and went back to the hematologist. He gave me more iron, but told me that he would not give me any more after that until I found out how I was losing blood. On my next visit to Houston, I made an appointment with my doctor. And after an exam and some discussion, he suspected that I may be losing blood in my stomach or intestines during times of stress. So, he prescribed a daily dose of antacid and that seemed to solve the problem. To date, my anemia problem has not resurfaced.

Within a few days of feeling better, Adela and I headed out for a trip to Houston to attend my friend Marc's wedding. We were about a mile from the airport when a man abruptly pulled in front of me and stopped. I hit him with my truck. When the police arrived, they quickly determined that it was the other man's fault, but still scheduled a court hearing for the next day. I explained we were on our way to the U.S. for a wedding, but they would not reschedule. The next day, to put it behind us quickly, we made a financial settlement with the other driver in court. We put our truck in the shop for repairs and that began a three-month ordeal with the truck in and out of the repair shop correcting defective and unfinished repair work.

Not surprisingly, people began to question why I was having so many trials. Even a parent of one of our students, a pastor, came to ask if his daughter may be committing some sin that might be causing all the trials for me and the ministry. I assured him that his daughter was a good girl and although it seemed to everyone that the wrath of God was being released on me, the truth was that we had received far more blessings than trials. Most of our students were doing well in school and growing spiritually and we were now almost completely out of debt. Life was good, a little inconvenient at times, but very good overall. But our biggest trial was still to come.

On September 30th, I was returning home from Houston and about halfway home on the drive from the airport in San Pedro Sula. I got a late start and it was beginning to get dark. I rarely drive after dark because it is very dangerous, because of poorly marked roads and bandits. But I had a boy, Mica, with me who was coming to visit our ministry and wanted to get him to our house. We had just refueled in Trinidad and I remember telling Mica how I hated driving at dusk because it's difficult to see.

It wasn't dark enough for headlights to do any good, so I was driving very slowly. As we approached the Chinda turnoff, there was a bus stopped at a bend in the road there. Its rear lights were bright and flashing so I pulled into the oncoming lane to see if it was clear to go around the bus. Immediately I saw what I thought were two motorcycles turning in my direction from the Chinda road, so I pulled back into my lane. There was a power failure in Chinda at that time, so the street lights were out which made it very difficult to see.

The first oncoming motorcycle passed me with no problem, it turned out to be a moto taxi, (a three-wheeled taxi). The other motorcycle was a typical two-wheeler, carrying a passenger. For some reason, the driver lost control and laid the cycle down. It was sliding out of control right at my truck. It was moving very erratically so it was hard to tell what I should do to avoid it. It was on my side of the road, so I had to move to the left to try to avoid it. I had almost come to a stop when it slid under my truck, hitting me on the passenger's side front wheel.

People immediately started coming from everywhere, some trying to help and others just to see what had happened. By now it was very dark. I started getting out of my vehicle to see the two men under my truck. People were yelling at me to pull forward because my wheel was on top of one of them. So, I pulled forward and the bystanders then pulled the two men out. They loaded them into the back of a pickup truck and took them to the hospital in Santa Barbara about fifteen or twenty minutes away. Both men looked like they were in very bad shape. Some of the bystanders had moved the motorcycle to the side of the road and I told them to move it back until the police arrived. They moved it back, but it was impossible to put it where it had originally been.

My truck remained where it was after I had pulled forward, in the middle of the road straddling the centerline. While we were waiting for the police, a man named Geovany, who spoke a little English, told me that he had witnessed the accident and the motorcycle had lost control because he had hit the bus. I told him that I didn't speak any Spanish, so he sent for a young lady who lived only a few hundred yards from the accident. In about ten minutes, Celia arrived. Her English wasn't great, but she was a help.

After a few more minutes, the Trinidad police arrived. They said that the accident was in Santa Barbara's jurisdiction, so they couldn't do anything until police from Santa Barbara got there. Fortunately, they stayed and secured the scene, because a few minutes later we got word that the motorcycle passenger was dead, and the driver was paralyzed. When that word went through the crowd, some started getting hostile and threatened to kill me. The Trinidad police put my passenger, Mica, Celia and me in one of the police trucks and posted police with machine guns around the truck. The people were trying to turn the truck over and I could tell by the looks on the policemen's faces, they were concerned that things would get beyond what they could control. Fortunately, the Santa Barbara police soon arrived, which put about a dozen or more police at the scene. I probably owe my life to the Trinidad police. God clearly used them to protect me.

We remained at the accident site for about an hour while the Santa Barbara police did their investigation. Then we were taken to the impoundment lot to store the vehicles and then to the Santa Barbara police station. I was in shock, I knew I had done nothing wrong, but the thought that I was involved in the death of a person was beyond description. I can't compare it to anything I'd ever experienced. I called Adela to tell her to come immediately, then I called a friend whose brother-in-law was high up in Honduran government and told her I needed help. I gave my statement to the Santa Barbara Police through Celia. It was very basic because of her limited English skills. Adela arrived at about 9:00 PM and they let her take Mica, and all our luggage to our student apartment in Santa Barbara where she spent the night. The Santa Barbara apartment was one that we rented for our students who attended classes in Santa Barbara. The students had left to go back to La Union for the weekend, so it was available for Adela

I was charged with vehicular homicide and held at the police station for arraignment the next day. Fortunately, the call I had made earlier had initiated a call from her brother-in-law to the Santa Barbara Police, directing them to detain me, but not to put me in jail.

Thank God, I shudder to think what a night in the Santa Barbara jail in the general population would have been like. I spent the night in one of the police station offices.

I had a serious time of prayer that night in that office and with the help of the Holy Spirit, I was convinced that this was all from God's hand. I had a peace about that and at about 10:30 PM I fell asleep sitting up in an office chair and slept without waking up until 6:30 AM the next morning. Adela arrived about 7:00 AM and we tried to reach my lawyer, Juan. I call him my lawyer because he had done several title transfers for me for property purchases I'd made over the years. His home was in La Union, but he lived in Santa Barbara during the work week. We reached him, and he arrived about 8:00 AM.

We spent most of the day at the police station waiting to be arraigned. Finally, at about 5:30 PM, they took me to the court where I was arraigned, assigned a public defender, scheduled for court on October 30th and released. If you've ever been arrested for anything in your home country, even for something as minor as a parking ticket, you know it's a nerve-wracking experience. But being arrested in a foreign country where you don't know the language or the process, it's worse than your most terrible nightmare.

As we began to prepare for the trial, I became very frustrated in my inability to connect and communicate with the public defender. I couldn't use Juan as my lawyer because he was also a Santa Barbara judge. I'm obviously not a lawyer, so I had no choice but to continue with the public defender. Celia located several witnesses, but because of fear of retaliation, only two were willing to come forward to testify. On October 30th, the morning of the trial, I had to find the witnesses and bring them to court. Their names were Filipa and Geovanni. Giovanni was the man I talked to the night of the wreck.

The trial was not in a normal courtroom like I expected, but in a big open room with about eight meeting areas. That was the Honduran court system. The only people in each meeting area were the judge, the defendants, the accusers and the lawyers. Everyone else waited outside until they were called in. My friend Laura could be my translator and sit with me. Laura Handel had worked for me for several years when we were in the early stages of designing and building the mission base. She is an architect who was also very helpful as a translator with our construction workers. We became good friends and she continues to help me with translations of all kinds. The judge first heard from the policeman who was the primary accident investigator and his findings in the wreck were totally wrong. He didn't even mention the bus, and his whole opinion of what happened was based on the fact that my truck was found to be straddling the centerline of the road. In his opinion, that put me totally at fault.

I had been in two previous wrecks in Honduras. Both had been in San Pedro Sula. In both cases, I was extremely impressed by the accuracy of the accident investigator's findings. But this investigator was totally wrong. Fortunately, both eye-witnesses were strong, definite and convincing about what they saw. As a result, the judge rendered a not guilty verdict.

I was overjoyed. But my joy turned back to frustration when I was told that the district attorney had filed an appeal. I felt that everyone at the trial was convinced of my innocence by the strength of the witnesses, but I learned later that the driver of the motorcycle had a highly-placed relative in the Honduras government and the government official had pressured the district attorney to appeal.

Several months later I was told that the verdict had been overturned and I was going to be sentenced soon. At that point, it was obvious that something was going on behind closed doors. The appeal judges didn't want to talk to the witnesses or look at any evidence, they just overturned the verdict.

I had been working with another lawyer in Tegucigalpa on some filings for the ministry and he spoke English. I called him and told him what had happened. He suggested that we file a motion with the Supreme Court that my rights had been violated. I agreed, and we proceeded. When the Santa Barbara court was notified that I had filed a motion with the Supreme Court, they changed their verdict reversal and decided to give me a new trial in 2018. So, we sit and wait.

I'm confident that once again I will be found innocent. Several months ago, as I prayed, I felt God reveal that I shouldn't worry because this ordeal was not about me. He was going to use my case to reveal himself to the judiciary of Honduras. But for now, they are still holding my truck for evidence and I'm not allowed to drive until a final verdict is rendered. I remain confident that this is all from God's hand and as we wait, I rarely think much about it except in my daily prayers.

Chapter Twenty-Eight
Life Levels Off

Other than the pending trial hanging out there, life seemed to level off. God continued to be faithful in meeting our financial needs and we entered 2017 debt free. We also had enough money to complete our *OANSA* building and improve the infrastructure of the mission base. This was especially important because city water had become less and less reliable as the town had grown. We went as many as three days without water. So, we added storage tanks with a capacity to hold a week's supply of water.

Our students continue to flourish spiritually and academically. They have become more and more adept in their management of the *OANSA* program. We have even expanded the program, adding a soccer competition one afternoon a week.

Some of the students were doing so well that we started a ministry counsel, comprised of Adela, me, and six of our most spiritually advanced students. We meet at least once a week to discuss issues within the ministry and they help us make most ministry decisions. We also meet one morning a week for prayer.

We have Sunday morning church services in the mission base that are open to the community. The students lead the worship and prayer portion of the service, and I give the message through our translator, Estela. The third Sunday of each month is designated as primarily a youth service. The students prepare and perform a drama during that service.

As we enter 2018, most of us feel the need to grow spiritually stronger, so the students have established a prayer group that meets Tuesday and Thursday mornings, 4:00 AM – 5:00 AM; and Sunday mornings from 5:00 AM – 6:00 PM.

As we finished our seventh public school year of ministry in November of 2017, we're proud to have helped five students graduate from high school We currently have three students in the university and three more students ready to start university prep school in February. And our oldest girl, Edita, has been accepted as an intern at a prominent law firm in Tegucigalpa to start in January where she will work while finishing her law degree.

Most of our students truly believe that God has a plan for their life to change the world around them as they travel life's journey. They believe this because they are seeing it happen in theirs and the lives of the other students around them. Three of our most mature students who have expressed the desire to join the staff of our ministry upon completion of their education. Finally, after a two-year effort, our new website is up and running, www.honduraschristianyouthmissions.org

Chapter Twenty-Nine
What About the Monsters?

In the previous chapters, I've tried to share that prior to moving to Honduras I've experienced many seasons of God's blessings, joy, and peace. But since the inception of this ministry to students, I am experiencing an ongoing continuous confidence and peace that I'm doing exactly what God had planned for my life. Don't get me wrong, living in a third world country can supply its share of frustrating moments. *But the peace of knowing I am on God's preordained path inspires me to thank God every day for the privilege of being part of His ministry here.*

Do I feel like I've arrived or achieved spiritual maturity? No, I think I've just begun to scratch the surface of learning what God really has for us. But I do think that in my 39 years of being a Christian I've finally begun to understand the battle, and what it takes to be victorious over all the opposition we face on the journey to becoming children of God. Do I consider myself a Bible scholar? No, not by any recognized standards, but I've read the Bible from cover to cover approximately 30 times, and the New Testament over 100 times in my daily quiet times. That doesn't count the additional time I've spent in the scriptures studying or preparing messages. As a result, I think God has given me an understanding of what the Bible says and what God expects of us.

Finally, I'm by no means a psychologist. But my life's journey and recovery work have revealed several behavior defects that I have and how I can achieve victory over them. These obstacles, powers, oppositions, and behavior defects are what I call *monsters*. But no matter what you or I choose to call them, they must be conquered to find the life of Kingdom peace, joy and power that God wants for us, and most of those victories must be won from within.

Over the years, as I've read and pondered Galatians 2:20, *"I have been crucified with Christ and I no longer live, but Christ lives in me. The life I live in the body, I live by faith in the Son of God, who loved me and gave Himself for me."* I understand that Paul is discussing gaining freedom from the law through Christ, but in his proclamation, he has also inspired me to set a primary goal and daily prayer for myself to achieve. It is that "I (with the help of God) need to crucify all of my old self and all its natural and sinful desires so that the fullness of Christ is free to live in me. When that is accomplished, I feel I can confidently walk in the faith that He is in control of my every thought, word, and action." The process of seeking that goal guarantees there will be a significant battle.

As I write this book, I feel that God is continually impressing on me the importance of understanding the battle(s) we Christians face, and the monsters we must conquer in those battles. Before we talk further about the battle, I feel I need to lay the groundwork of what the Bible has taught me.

The primary message of the Bible is reconciliation, starting with our reconciliation with our Lord. Sin has caused a separation between us and the one and only Holy God. Romans 3:23 says, *"For all have sinned and fallen short of the glory of God."* And for that reason, God cannot fellowship with sin. The Bible teaches that God's top priority is reconciling the sin issue. John 3:16, *"For God so loved the world that He gave his only begotten Son, that whosoever believes in him shall not perish but have eternal life."* There is no other path to reconciliation with God other than accepting the gift of forgiveness that has been achieved through the crucifixion, death, burial, and resurrection of our Lord Jesus Christ, (John 14:6), Christ's sinless, voluntary submission and surrender to that process paid the penalties for our sins.

If we *honestly* believe that we are sinners needing a savior and recognize Jesus as God's provision of payment for our sins, and ask for and receive God's forgiveness, we are saved. Romans 10:9-10 says, *"That if you confess with your mouth, 'Jesus is Lord,' and believe in your heart that God raised Him from the dead, you will be saved. For it is with your heart that you believe and are justified, and it is with your mouth that you confess and are saved."*

I think most Christians would agree with me to this point. But now I ask a question that may be more difficult, how is it that scripture tells us that some of us will enter heaven to receive a reward, and others will enter heaven as one escaping flames (1 Corinthians 3:15-16)? And here's one more question. Since scripture says that *anyone* who has faith will do the things (miracles) that Jesus did and even greater things, why aren't Christians doing those things and performing miracles?

I know there are instances of miracles. We have seen some miraculous healings in Honduras because of our prayers. For example, one girl had multiple tumors in her breasts and they disappeared after we prayed. There was another girl so ill that the doctors had sent her home to die because they couldn't figure out what was wrong with her or what to do. When we prayed for her she looked like she was already dead. She had a greenish gray color that was horrifying. We prayed for her on a Sunday and on Tuesday, when we went back to check on her, she was fine.

There are others, but the point I'm trying to make is that although there are scattered miracles, I think scripture is implying that they should be more common among believers. Why isn't it? I'm convinced the answer to these questions and others like these has a lot to do with how far we've advanced in our journey to become God's children. After salvation, I think most Christians would agree, we move into a stage of sanctification. This is where the real battle begins. The dictionary tells us the term "sanctify" means to be reserved for sacred use, to consecrate, to purify or to be made holy. Ephesians 1:13-14 (and other scriptures) tell us that upon believing, we receive the Holy Spirit into our being as God's guarantee of our future inheritance.

The Holy Spirit is and will be the motivating force and enabling power through the rest of our lives as believers. He will be our primary connection to the Godhead, our teacher, our life-changer, our guide and our strength to name a few of the things He does for us.

I'm purposely not addressing the process of being born again and receiving the Spirit because there are several opinions on how and when that happens. What's most important is that receiving the Holy Spirit is part of the salvation process and the start of a lifelong process of sanctification.

John 1:12 is a passage that I can't let go of because it gives us one of the most exciting promises of the Bible. *"To those who received Him, to those who believed in His name, He gave the* right *to become children of God."* Believing in and receiving Christ gives us the *right* to become children of God. It's one of the most thought-provoking verses in scripture. What does that really mean? For sure it implies that we have a process of sanctification ahead of us, but what else? I think it's also an encouragement to prepare us for the battles that lie ahead on that journey. God wants us to know that no matter how hard the monsters try to discourage us and try to convince us we're out of our league, God has told us we have the *right* not only to be participants in the journey, but, we also have the *right* to be victorious in our battles all the way to the kingdom.

Philippians 1:6 tells us, *"being confident of this, that He who began a good work in you, will carry it on to completion until the day of Christ Jesus."* I believe this is telling us several things. I believe it confirms that God has a plan for your life and mine. I think this passage and 2 Peter 1:3-11 teach that the sanctification process is fundamentally the same for all of us, with the goal being to make us more like Christ. I think the path of that process may vary according to God's specific plan for each of us. If you combine Philippians 1:6, (which we've quoted above), with Psalm 139:16; *"your eyes saw my unformed body. All the days ordained for me were written in your book before one of them came to be."* And Ephesians 2:10; *"For we are God's workmanship, created in Christ Jesus to do good works, which God prepared in advance for us to do."* I think it becomes clear that God, in fact, does have a specific plan for each of our lives and that plan was designed and ordained before we were born.

While I'm sure God's plan includes our work life which is a means of positioning us for His purposes, I think He is more concerned with our spiritual maturity and usability in His Kingdom plan, wherever we have been positioned. To "sanctify" also means to set apart. This brings us to what I think is the second significant message of the Bible. God wants to have a personal, intimate relationship with each of us so that He can enjoy fellowship with us and use us in His plan just as He used Jesus to accomplish His objective while He was on earth. Now I'm not implying that we will ever be on a level with Jesus. He was God and He was sinless. But I believe Jesus' ministry as taught in the gospels teaches us that it is God's intention for us to have open communication with God the Father through the Holy Spirit. This is not only so that He can teach us through the scriptures but also communicate with us to mold us and shape us to be like Jesus and guide us in specific situations.

I'm not saying to expect that God will speak audibly, although I don't rule out His ability to do that. But He speaks to us intuitively. The Spirit spoke, (unclear whether this is audible or intuitive) to Phillip, (Acts 8:29, "Go to the chariot of the eunuch"). He spoke to Peter in Acts 11:12, where Peter states, "The Spirit told me", and He spoke to Paul and others on numerous other occasions. We rightly study what God said to the apostles, but we seem to ignore the bigger issue that He did speak to them through His Spirit.

God regularly speaks to me intuitively, and I've confirmed that He does the same with many preachers, God directs them in their preparation and delivery of sermons. There have probably been a half-dozen times when God has spoken to me so clearly that I had to stop and look around to see where the voice came from. Please understand that I'm not trying to portray myself as a super saint. The point I feel called to make is that *God wants to speak to all His children, and He needs to speak to His children to carry out His Kingdom plan through them.* Sometimes it is subtle and intuitive, and at other times He speaks in an unmistakable, undeniable way.

Unfortunately, most Christians have not grown to know, recognize and hear the voice of God. I believe the reason for this is that most Christians, rather than choosing to fight and conquer the monsters obstructing our journey to Kingdom living by learning to use God's resources for victory, we have used the blessings of God to finance our detour around God's growth exercises (trials, challenges) giving the monsters a victory by default. This results in lives that lack the real sustained peace, joy, and power that they have been given the *right* to.

I thank God that since I came to Honduras and started serving in this ministry, God has allowed me (through my circumstances and lack of options to escape from trials), to know Him far more intimately than before. Once again, I'm not a super Christian. But I know that what I have learned and enjoyed in my relationship with God is available to all Christians and I want to communicate that. The better news is that I'm sure that God wants more for us than I can testify to experiencing, a lot more. In the last several years, by submitting to and trusting God, I have had victories over things (monsters) that I had struggled with for decades, and I'm now convinced that there are even more victories to come.

I am concerned about how many Christians are missing these blessings, and the chance to pass these joys to their children. From some of what I've written, you may ask "aren't you being awfully judgmental of Christians in general?" I'm not judging, I'm recognizing things that I've done myself, and know that there are others like me that are doing what I've done.

For example, I think back on when I was considering moving my family to Africa for my business venture there. One of my biggest concerns was that I might be depriving my youngest daughter Stacie of "the American high school experience." As I reflect on that concern, I marvel at how misguided my thinking was. I could have provided Stacie a much more enriching and God-focused lifestyle than that which the high school culture would have tempted her with. My friends who are currently in the parenting phase have been telling me some disheartening statistics. They report that 80-90% of students that have been brought up in Christian homes, move away from the church while they are in college. If these statistics are true, why are they true?

It is because many parents aren't pursuing an intimate relationship with God. They may be Christians, they go to church and church functions and do church things. They don't smoke, drink or do drugs, all of which are good Christian lifestyle behaviors, but a deeper relationship with God is not a priority to them. In our culture, we get caught up in the business of life and have no time left to pursue God in scripture and prayer. And it's only logical and easy to understand that to have a good relationship with anyone requires spending time together.

I first saw this phenomenon in the 90s, when I led a study on the disciplines of Christianity. One of the assignments in our study was to survey our *Christian* friends about their quiet times, (regular times spent in Bible reading, meditation, and prayer). One of our surprising findings was that fewer than five percent of those we surveyed, reported that they had any kind of daily time with God.

As parents, we can only teach our kids what we ourselves know. Our children will naturally develop their habits and beliefs based on the strongest influences around them. If we pursue a real relationship with God and teach your children to do so, they will not stray. (Proverbs 22:6)

In our Honduran ministry to students, our number one goal is to teach them how to establish and nurture a relationship with God. We know that we can give them the information, but we can't make them use it. But we can let them see it in our lives. And we are seeing results. For our students who do pursue that relationship, which many do, we are seeing amazing things coming from their lives and as their education progresses, they are showing no interest in abandoning their sacred relationship with the Lord.

Over the years, I've examined the sanctification process, as described in 2 Peter 1:3-11, which says:

> *His divine power has given us everything we need for life and godliness through our knowledge of Him who called us by his own glory and goodness. Through these, He has given us his very great and precious promises, so that through them you may participate in the divine nature and escape the corruption in the world caused by evil desires. For this very reason, make every effort to add to your faith goodness; and to goodness, knowledge; and to knowledge, self-control; and to self-control, perseverance; and to perseverance, godliness; to godliness, brotherly kindness; and to brotherly kindness, love. For if you possess these qualities in*

increasing measure, they will keep you from being ineffective and unproductive in your knowledge of our Lord Jesus Christ. But if anyone does not have them, he is nearsighted and blind, and has forgotten that he has been cleansed from his past sins. Therefore, my brothers, be all the more eager to make your calling and election sure. For if you do these things, you will never fall, and you will receive a rich welcome into the eternal kingdom of our Lord and Savior Jesus Christ.

Several things in this passage have impressed me. First is the statement in Verse 3 that God's power has given us *everything* we need for life and godliness. This passage is promising us that Jesus is sufficient for everything we need from the basics of life to our level of spiritual maturity when we allow the Holy Spirit to be in control of our life. (I'll come to godliness again in a minute.)

Verse 4 tells us that God's promises are to enable us to escape the corruption of the worldly culture and participate in the divine nature, which is another way of saying enjoy a life of walking in godliness. The passage goes on to tell us that we need to add to our faith, goodness; to goodness, knowledge; to knowledge, self-control; to self-control, perseverance; to perseverance, godliness; to godliness, brotherly kindness; and to brotherly kindness, love.

The thing I wrestled with for years is the part of the passage that starts with goodness and ultimately leads to godliness. I've spent a lot of time researching this, and I find that goodness is behaving or doing what's right because I *know* it's right, which means, I am usually using self-control to do it. Unfortunately, my self-control doesn't always prevail, especially when no one is looking.

Godliness, on the other hand, is behaving because *it has become my nature* to do right. Jesus wasn't sinless because He was self-controlled, He behaved the way He did because it was His nature. From what I've learned and experienced, the difference between goodness and godliness is what makes the difference between a lukewarm, ineffective Christian or church to being one who is powerful and effective.

Earlier in this chapter, I talked about Paul's proclamation in Galatians 2:20, where he claimed to no longer live, but that Christ lived in him. I believe that Paul was proclaiming what it is like to have reached the level of godliness. With God's help the man Paul had once been, along with the bad within him, had been crucified with Christ; and most, if not all the monsters he had battled had been conquered as well. Now he was free to allow Christ, who has taken over who he was to be in control of all he was. He no longer had to fight the major battles of right and wrong because the nature of Christ was now in control and he could walk in the faith of that fact. He wasn't saying he was perfect, but that he had surrendered himself sufficiently to God that Jesus was now the pilot of his body.

Based on my experience and what I see in scripture, I believe most Christians never get beyond the sanctification level of goodness, because we're not willing to face and conquer the trials and challenges that lie in the stage of perseverance.

Let's talk about battling those "monsters" in us. There are lots of foes to battle in our sanctification journey; the devil and his demons, our fleshly nature, our habits, our desires, our incorrect beliefs, our prejudices, our behavior defects and more. But I don't think it matters which of these we are trying to conquer, the Bible teaches that our first line of defense is our relationship with God, being able to hear His voice and being obedient to His direction.

That sounds simple, but the Bible teaches that there are many evil powers in the universe that are trying to prevent that. But the good news is, that if we are obedient to scripture and follow God's instruction, we can overcome those forces and those monsters we may have nurtured within us. As a result, we all can have a victorious and amazing, kingdom life, a life of peace, joy, and fulfillment enjoying and bearing the fruit of the spirit.

In this battle, one of the first things that we need to recognize is that our culture has taken over and is misguiding us in who we are and what we should be doing. The contemporary cultural script for life is, get an education, establish a career, raise a family, plan for retirement and retire comfortably. We rely on hard work, excellence, diligence, creativity, and tenacity to achieve these goals. For

Christians, while we're doing those things, we try to honor God by behaving ourselves during the process. We participate in Bible studies or do ministry work as an additional activity along the way. But for many, God and one's relationship with Him are not priorities, and get overlooked in our pursuit of our culturally-driven plans.

Remember my encounter with God that I shared in an earlier chapter when dealing with Lola. My feisty neighbor who hated me. God said, "I don't care how creative, hard-working or clever you are, I (God) am the only one who knows what has to happen in Lola's life for her to become a Christian." If we are going to be effective in changing the world around us, we must be able to function at a level with God where he can, in fact, direct us in ministering to the lives in that world. We need to be living at a level of godliness that gives the fullness of Christ full reign in our thoughts, our words and our actions. I was only able to change Lola, by hearing and obeying God's direction. Only God knew what Lola needed to see, hear and experience to change who she was. As God directed me and as I was obedient, Lola was converted.

> *God did not save us just, so we can go to heaven, He saved us so that He can make us like Christ and use us on a preplanned and ordained life's journey to change the world around us. At home, at school, at work, at the cleaners, at the store, in the community and in our church, God wants to sanctify us and develop the character of Christ in us and communicate with us in all those situations so that He can use us to be His influence, His ambassadors in all those capacities.*

We need to put behind us the cultural wisdom or the notion that we can be effective Christians because we are cleverer, more excellent, more charming, more hard-working, more creative or more tenacious than the world. The only way we are going to be what God wants us to be and change the world for the kingdom will be by God's direction using His wisdom, His methods, and His resources.

Chapter Thirty
The Process

I don't consider myself a poster child for Christianity, But as I stated, I feel that I've learned how to win many of the battles we face on the journey and I'd like to share what I've learned. The most important thing I have learned is that I need to make knowing, hearing and talking to God my priority. All else comes after that.

I also want to state emphatically, that although we're talking a lot about hearing God's voice, God's primary means of communication with us is through His Word, the scriptures. They are foundational and all other communication with God must be built on and in harmony with the Bible.

The Bible clearly tells us, that God needs to be our priority. In Matthew 6:31-33, Jesus tells us that if we seek first God's Kingdom and His righteousness, He will take care of all our needs. I don't think He's telling us to quit our jobs, but I see this as telling us to make sure that we make a time of fellowship with God every day our top priority. By committing to having a time with God every day we are putting Him first and taking the initiative to further the sanctification process, adding to our faith, goodness, as written in 2 Peter1:5.

It is best when we do this first thing each day. Get up and practice the disciplines of Christianity. Read your Bible, (I'd recommend that you don't start in Genesis, but start in John or another New Testament book. That'll be easier to understand and relate to as you get going), meditate on scripture, (think, pray and reflect about what you've read), memorize scripture, read a devotional and pray. I know that sounds like a lot. You don't start by trying to do everything. Start by just reading some scripture and praying. Pray for understanding before you read and pray for the wisdom to apply what you've read when you're finished.

This will be a big change to establish this new daily habit. The first and best step is to commit to do it for a specified amount of time each day, *with no days off.* You may say, "I'll have to get up earlier, and I already have a hard time getting up in the morning." I understand. You might identify that as the first monster on your list that needs to be defeated. I was not a morning person when I started, but I now find the early morning hours to be the most exciting time of my day. You might start by praying every night that God will wake you up the next morning and give you the strength to get out of bed. Remember, there is an enemy that wants you to stay in bed. But with God's help, you can overcome that. It's a decision. But if you make the decision to pray every night to get up in the morning, you are now fighting the battle with God on your side, and on the way to slaying your first monster. And it will be slain.

It will take some effort, and it may require more than one re-start, but with God's help, you will do it. Once you are routinely getting up early, pray about what God would have you do during that time. My normal routine is prayer for understanding, reading a devotional, (*My Utmost for His Highest,* by Oswald Chambers, is my favorite), meditating on that, then reading my Bible, and meditating on that as I read. Then I might do some specific Bible study or read from a Christian book or publication, I love Christian biographies. Then I pray.

For daily Bible reading, I would suggest three or four chapters a day. You can read through the entire Bible in less than a year reading four chapters a day. It's a good idea to mix your reading with Old and New Testaments because there are sections of the Old Testaments that can get dry, especially the first time through it. But over time, you begin to see how it all fits together, Old Testament and New, and it will inspire a greater hunger to know it better and deeper.

I don't want to scare you, but in 1992 I started my quiet time. It took two re-starts. But once I got going, I started spending about ten to twenty minutes each morning, and now I try to spend at least an hour, and at times, I might spend up to three hours. It's a lot like eating, you know when you're full. And for me, sometimes my hunger isn't satisfied until I've spent 2-3 hours. I'm reminded that an acorn seedling can survive on one tablespoon of water a day, but a full-grown oak tree consumes as much as 50 gallons of water a day. It has never been a goal to spend more and more time with God. But just like anything else, when you enjoy doing something, it can consume you and you become unaware of the time. That's me. My mornings with the Lord started out to be a chore, but in very short order, it became my favorite time of the day. Remember, our daily time with God should always include both reading scripture and praying. Then meditating on what we've read is extremely helpful once we've learned to focus and concentrate. Your quiet time will grow as you and your appetite for God grows... And it will.

When you make the commitment to that time with God every day, it will seem like a chore at first. But if you will stick with it and allow it to become a habit rather than a chore, God will begin to work in your heart, and you will gradually begin to appreciate and enjoy the time with God. Let me warn you, it could take up to ninety days for that to happen, so be patient, and try to be conscious of your heart condition. God communicates best through a humble heart and a contrite spirit (Isaiah 66:2).

When your time with God becomes regular and becomes a part of you, God will begin to reveal insights to you through scripture. He will convict you of sin in your life that needs to be addressed. He will direct you to sources of knowledge which will, in turn, direct you as to how He wants to use you. If you're like me, God will reveal things to you during your time with Him that you will be sure are coming from God, but for the rest of the day, you will be bombarded with "common sense" thoughts that contradict those insights.

You'll have to learn to trust the insights that you feel are coming from God rather than your common sense, (Proverbs 3:5-6), *"Trust in the Lord with all your heart and lean not on your own understanding; in all your ways acknowledge Him, and He will make your paths straight."* There is nothing wrong with questioning what you think God is telling you, God wants us to ask for wisdom, (James 1:5-6), *"If any of you lacks wisdom, he should ask God, who gives generously to all without finding fault, and it will be given to him. But when he asks, he must believe and not doubt, because he who doubts is like a wave of the sea, blown and tossed by the wind."*

As the passage says, at some point you must step out on what God is telling you. I promise God will not expect you to take any huge leaps of faith until you are ready, (Proverbs 19:2), *"It is not good to have zeal without knowledge, nor to be hasty and miss the way."*

As the quality of your time with God grows, your knowledge of God, (very important to embrace His promises), and His direction to other sources of knowledge will grow. As you grow, and your studies expand, it would be wise to invest in a good Bible dictionary, an exhaustive concordance, a Bible commentary and a comparative study Bible. You will now also find that you are moving forward in the progression of sanctification, as described in (2 Peter 1:5) by adding to goodness, knowledge. As you progress in your journey, the monsters and their attacks will become bigger and stronger. But God allows that for a good reason. We can't grow unless our challenges become bigger and tougher. That's how athletes train, by facing tougher and tougher opponents. But always remember the promise of 1 Corinthians 10:13, *"No temptation has seized you except what is common to man. And God is faithful, He will not allow you to be tempted beyond what you can bear. But when you are tempted, He will also provide a way out so that you can stand up under it."*

This passage is dealing with temptation to sin, but the temptation to abandon the journey can turn out to be a sin with catastrophic consequences. God will not allow you to be tempted or challenged beyond what you can bear. Some may think I'm taking liberty in my interpretation, but as I've prayed about it, I don't think so. At this point, God is beginning to teach you self-control (2 Peter 1:6). As God stretches us in the use of our faith, goodness, knowledge, and self-control, and *if we are committed to holding the course*, we will eventually come to the end of ourselves. We will have used all the natural or fleshly tools that we have used to survive and excel in our natural lives, but they cannot take us any further.

If we're to grow spiritually beyond this point, we must learn to depend on God, His promises and His resources to continue. We have reached the point of spiritual poverty referred to in (Matthew 5:3*), "Blessed are the poor in spirit, for theirs is the kingdom of heaven."* I'm convinced that this is the threshold of the Kingdom.

Until now, we have pretty much been using natural tools of character that we were born with. Tools that we have learned to use and depend on in our natural lives. But from this point forward they are worthless. In fact, if we try to use them in the challenges of the perseverance stage of sanctification, they can be a major handicap.

I understand that self-control, which we normally would consider a natural attribute, is listed as the step after knowledge, but I don't believe it is meant to be used in the same way as we've been accustomed to using it. I believe it's telling us to use self-control to hold the course through the trials of perseverance. *Unfortunately, this is where most Christians decide the hope of the journey's destination is not worth the perceived hardship of the journey.* But for those of us who have chosen to stay in the battle, we find that after the initial failures of trying to fight the new battles with the old weapons we learn to use the new weapons, the weapons in God's arsenal, and life becomes more exciting than ever. It becomes indescribable. But you have to be ready and be totally committed to the journey or the monsters will chew you up and spit you out before you get there.

As I try to think of an analogy, I know that nothing can compare with an intimate walk with God, but whitewater rafting comes to mind. Simply put, the rush of surviving the dangerous white waters is beyond comparison, but if your focus on the challenge lapses for a split second, you'll be in the raging waters and could be killed. But if we keep at it, God will bring us to a point where we learn how to let Him identify and fight our battles for us, (Ephesians 6:10-12). He'll bring us to a point where we must be purified in our relationship with Him to remove the obstacles to His working within us and His communication with us so that we are enabled to clearly hear his directions (Psalm 66:18) and (1 Peter 1:6-9). Finally, we must learn to trust in Him and surrender to Him by taking every thought captive and making it obedient, (2 Corinthians 10:3-5).

Learning those things will allow us to take our place in Christ's triumphant procession, (2 Corinthians 2:14-16).

Simply put, moving from goodness to godliness, is the transformation from us being in control of our lives to God being in control of our lives. (Galatians 2:20) *To get from operating in goodness, to the spiritual maturity level of godliness, we will have to embrace difficulty rather than run from it and experience the perseverance process. We must see every trial, challenge or disappointment as a learning experience and opportunity from the loving hand of God.*

James 1:4 tells us, *"Perseverance must finish its work so that you may be mature and complete, not lacking anything."* God has forced me to develop the habit of telling myself in every encounter containing any measure of challenge in life that, God loves me, God is Sovereign, and therefore, nothing can happen to me that is not from the hand of God and for my own good. *I promise you that, developing that thought pattern will change your life.* It changed mine. James 1:12 says, *"Blessed is the man who perseveres under trial, because when he has stood the test, he will receive the crown of life that God has promised to those who love Him."*

One of the key purposes of the Old Testament is to give us insights into God's relationships with His people. I know they operated under "the law" and we operate under grace because of the work of Jesus, and we have the Holy Spirit and they didn't, except on specific occasions. But God's love for His people and His desire for fellowship with them has always been the same.

If we study how God worked in the lives of Abraham, Jacob, Joseph and many others, we can see God's revealing His heart towards us. The story of Job is a good example of how God uses trials to refine us and enhance our relationship with Him. In the first two chapters of Job, we have the privilege of listening in on a conversation between God and the devil concerning one of God's beloved children, Job. It's exciting to see that God has a hedge of protection around Job, which tells me that we have a similar protection. It's also reassuring to know that the devil knows his place. He doesn't even ask permission to attack Job until God offers him up. God brags about what a good man Job is but for some reason, God allows the devil to bring a series of trials into Job's life. These are no small trials, they are painful and devastating.

But God has a plan, He doesn't share His purpose with the devil, but in God's wisdom, He knows that although Job is a good man, he does have a flaw. What's also comforting is that God knows exactly what level of pressure to allow the devil to apply to reveal and remove the flaw. In Job's discourse in chapters 26 through 31, Job reveals a significant sin issue of pride, (primarily in chapters 27, 29 and 31). After God allows Job to speak his piece and exhaust his self-proclaimed wisdom, God speaks in chapters 36 through 41. We hear the words of a wise, firm but loving father, which settles the issue of Jobs pride. We then hear Job's "prideless" reply, in Job 42:1-5, most significantly verse 5, *"My ears had heard of you, but now my eyes have seen you. Therefore, I despise myself and repent in dust and ashes."* Job didn't embrace the perseverance process, but God's plan of purification of Job's character was accomplished.

In another book of the Bible, the prophetic writing of Habakkuk illustrates the struggles we have when growing from a spiritual mentality of seeing and trying to understand things at face value to the maturity of trusting God despite what we see. It's a big leap that can only be achieved by God forcing us to persevere through trials. Habakkuk begins weeping and complaining because of what he sees, (Habakkuk 1:2), but his understanding grows, and he closes in praise and adoration stating his new desire and ability to trust God in spite of what he sees, (Habakkuk 3:16-19).

We mature to the level of Godliness only through persevering through trials and watching God prove himself faithful. We have a responsibility in the process of our sanctification. In Philippians 2:12-15 we are directed to work out our salvation with fear and trembling. Those who choose to be obedient to that direction can count on a season(s) of hardship, but if we persevere, we will fulfill the call and right to "become children of God" (Verse 15).

I'd also like to recommend a study of the eighth chapter of Romans. I believe it also gives us another perspective on how that new creation that we've become as Christians, (2 Corinthians 5:17), grows and becomes sanctified. When we choose to make decisions of obedience to the Holy Spirit, we mature and become stronger, but when we give in to the temptations inspired by our flesh, the devil and the other monsters we digress in the journey.

I've not said much about the last two stages of the sanctification process which are brotherly kindness and love primarily because although our ministry here to the youth of Honduras is a ministry that is both inspired and sustained by brotherly kindness and God's love, this is still new territory for me. I'm beginning to understand that both brotherly kindness and love take us to an even higher level of maturity and surrender, but I don't want to make statements that I'm not totally confident in. In fact, although I feel I operate at the level of godliness most of the time, I know I still have some white waters of perseverance to navigate before I'm there all the time.

When I reluctantly began this ministry, I didn't even have a love for children other than my own children and grandchildren. But as I was obedient to God and persevered through the first several months, God gradually developed in me a love for these kids a unique love for each of them that is indescribable. I have a special love that seems to be crafted by God in a special way to fit each one uniquely and individually. I'll say it again, I thank God every day for the privilege of serving in this ministry.

Chapter Thirty-One
Counseling and Celebrate Recovery

Getting help made a big difference for me. As you progress on your spiritual journey, it may come to light that you need help or counseling in the battle with some of your monsters. I believe that *all* our monsters have a spiritual element, but some are in the form of character flaws or behavioral defects and may need to be addressed through counseling. I have been to a few counselors over the past 35 years to deal with issues in my marriage and in more recent years to deal with the issues I've come to understand as codependency. Some counselors have helped me tremendously, others not so much. I would guess that there have been more than a dozen counselors that I've met with. All I can say is be careful.

I am not a psychologist or anything close to it. But I've spent enough time in counseling and around others with counseling experiences, that I've learned some things. Many of the monsters we face are considered by the world to be non-spiritual behavior defects and need to be dealt with by secular doctors. *But as Christians, we are spiritual beings who need to be counseled by a counselor with a Bible in one hand and their psychology book in the other. In other words, someone who will recognize our spiritual nature and approach helping us primarily from a Christian and or spiritual perspective.*

Of the counselors, I've spent time with, (all of whom called themselves Christian counselors), I think only two were qualified to deal with me and my issues. Both used the Bible as their primary foundation to get me on solid ground and to help me deal with my issues. If you choose to go to counseling, don't be afraid to keep trying new counselors until you find someone who is going to help you on both the spiritual and physical planes. But, even though I was helped by the two counselors I mentioned, I think I can honestly say that I saw more progress and growth by attending and applying what I learned in the recovery program.

I mentioned in an earlier chapter a program called *Celebrate Recovery* and how its Christ-centered twelve-step program helped me identify and solve issues that may have been the biggest monsters that I've had to deal with on my Christian journey. While the Bible doesn't specifically talk about issues like codependency, it does talk about the sufficiency of Christ in dealing with all our life's issues, (Luke 4:18-21). If Jesus can make the blind see, He can certainly deliver you from behavioral issues or whatever internal monsters we may be dealing with. I can testify that He has delivered me from codependency and several other issues. But I had to want to be delivered.

For example, for many years, and many times I tried to quit smoking without success. One day, God gave me a good reason to quit and I did. In December of 1981, I was still a new Christian and very enthusiastic. I was on my way to a Christmas party for my wife's work. I knew that people would ask me why I wasn't drinking, so I prayed and asked God for a response that would glorify Him. I intuitively heard, "tell them that my love for the people around me is stronger than my desire to drink, I just want to be a good example." That sounded like a good spiritual response to me, so I anxiously waited for my opportunity to use it.

As we ate dinner, I could hear the woman on the other side of my wife comment to my wife that I wasn't drinking. I said to myself, "Here's my chance." But before I could speak up, my wife said that "John thinks it's not glorifying to God to drink." The woman's response was, "Then why does he still smoke?" Boy was I convicted! At that very moment, I put out the cigarette that I was smoking and have never lit another. In an instant, I went from being a four pack a day smoker, who had smoked for twenty years, to a non-smoker. Somehow, I think as a result of my decision, God instantly removed my desire to smoke. Because I didn't struggle at all with the desire to smoke from that day forward.

During the two years I spent going through the Celebrate Recovery twelve-step program, (I went through it twice), I came to realize how many wounded Christians that there are out there. Many are struggling to overcome codependency, addictions, broken relationships and other related issues, but have had nowhere to turn for help. They had been too embarrassed to go to counseling and wouldn't or couldn't turn to their churches for fear of being judged or worse. As I dealt with my issues and listened to many others in my groups, I began to recognize common denominators that I saw in other Christians in the grip of a monster of their own. They desperately need help, but deny it, convincing themselves that they are perfectly fine, or that they can handle it on their own. They are afraid to admit otherwise. And without help, they remain in bondage.

As I wrote earlier, for God to move us to a level of maturity where He can use us to impact the world around us, He has to purify who we are. That includes overcoming not only our sin issues, but our character flaws and dysfunctional behavior as well. I think most people associate twelve-step programs with alcoholism and drug addiction. That's not totally incorrect. Many programs were originally designed to deal with those addictions, but there are several people struggling with debilitating dysfunctions in their relationships and attitudes, and the number of those people is much larger than those in the substance abuse groups.

In *Celebrate Recovery*, this need is identified as "life issues," and there are groups and instructions to help people identify and recover from non-addiction monsters, such as relationship issues. The program can help us restore and thrive in our marriages and family relationships, in our relationships with friends, our neighbors and at work. *Celebrate Recovery's* Christ-centered lessons help us realize who we are, what our dysfunctional tendencies are, how to replace those tendencies with healthy behaviors, and maybe most importantly, the encouraging realization that we are not the only one struggling with the problems we have.

One of the best outcomes of a program like *Celebrate Recovery* is that while in the program, we develop new kinds of friends, lifelong friends to love us, encourage us and hold us accountable to our recovery commitments. But like anything else, we will get out of it what we put into it.

It works, but it's not a magic pill. If we are not practicing the disciplines of Christianity that I mentioned earlier, while going through the program, the results will be far short of what they could have been. I've met people who have been attending various recovery meetings for years, but without experiencing any real difference in their lives. On the other hand, I have seen those who seriously want change, who have combined the *Celebrate Recovery* step study with their daily time with God, who have experienced an amazing change in their lives and spiritual maturity. My friend Marc is one of those. He and I have become real friends since we met in the *Celebrate Recovery* step study. He has turned around his wrecked life and gone on to be Director of one of the Texas *Celebrate Recovery* programs. He continues to be one of my best friends who encourages me, holds me accountable and is someone with whom I can discuss anything with without fear of judgment.

If you are struggling with issues that you don't feel you can safely discuss with anyone else, it would be well worth your time to visit a *Celebrate Recovery* meeting near you. *Celebrate Recovery* is a safe place because one of their strictest rules is about confidentiality. They have a saying; "What is said in the group, stays in the group." So, you can count on your privacy being respected, and you can let people know who you really are and what's really going on in your life.

There are tens of thousands of *Celebrate Recovery* groups meeting all over the world, so I'm sure you can find a group near you. Visit their website to locate the most convenient meeting, www.celebraterecovery.com.

Chapter Thirty-Two
Where Do We Go from Here?

Adela and I plan to continue our journey here in Honduras, equipping youth to be world changers by God's direction. He has given us a bold and a bit scary vision for 2018, but that only means we will hopefully finish the year stronger than we started. In November of 2017, as I finished my last steel business project, I felt God impress on me that at least for the near future He wants us to trust Him totally for all the ministry funding. If you remember, for the past three years God has used our Houston steel projects to supply most of our funding. So, yes, it's a scary vision to trust God for the needs of twenty-three people, but I think we're ready. God proved Himself faithful to about half-a-million-people wandering in the middle-eastern desert back in the days of Moses. Surely, He can and will take care of us.

In 2017 God impressed on me to set up a Honduras non-profit foundation to establish and own businesses that would help with the support of the ministry. Beyond supporting the ministry, these businesses will give us opportunities to train our students in trades for their future. We hope to have that foundation up and running in early 2018 when we plan to begin establishing a carpentry shop, an Aquaponics farm, (system of growing fish and vegetables together), and a small restaurant and hotel. We also feel like God wants us to open a school of our own, like an American homeschool. All this will require a higher level of surrender and trust. But, if we believe what we say we believe, we will hold tightly to it, and it will be an exciting year as God executes His plans.

As I reflect on my life and what I've written, it is my hope that my story has been successful in carrying two messages that may inspire you to action.

First, I hope that if you do not have a regular time with God, you will see the wisdom and understand the benefits of participating in a personal relationship with our loving heavenly Father daily. My hope is that you will be inspired to commit to that relationship for yourself. If you remember, I began a quiet time with God early on in my Christian life, and that was the beginning of an intimate relationship with God. You may also remember that I was incorrectly counseled at one point to spend more time with my wife and less time with God.

As a result, my life went in circles for ten years until I again started having a daily quiet time in 1992. God gave us the *right* as Christians (John 1:12), to experience a relationship with Him as the first disciples did. And when we enter that relationship, it will become so fulfilling that it radiates from our being as it did from theirs. When that happens the people and the world around us can't help but be changed. Won't you take God at His word and experience Him for yourself?

Secondly, my desire is that once you have a regular time with God, you would take bolder steps of obedience in answer to God's call to higher levels of surrender and participation in His kingdom.

For years before my moral failure, recovery and ministry in Honduras, I sensed God was telling me He wanted to take me to a new level of kingdom living, but because of my perceptions about my situations, responsibilities, and commitments, I never took God seriously, and I didn't seek His direction in reaching out for that new level of fellowship with Him. I was satisfied with the life that God had blessed me with through previous years of fellowship and obedience with Him not knowing that there was much more available. Scared of the risk of being taken out of my comfort zone, I never answered God's call.

But I can testify that, *once our relationship with God begins to be established*, God will only allow us to ignore His call to a higher level of spiritual maturity for so long before He forces us through trials and circumstances to answer His call to obedience (Philippians 1:6). In my case, He had to level me and allow my world to discard me to get me alone in a place with no options other than paying total attention to Him for some serious remedial training. I encourage you to heed God's call when it's given. He has wonders and possibilities to show you as well.

We need more than supernatural truth, and we need a supernatural mind to receive it.

1 Corinthians 2:11 (paraphrase)

God has supernatural plans and possibilities for us, but before He can reveal them to us, He must change and prepare us so that we are able to receive them. Are you ready to let God change you so you can take your rightful place as a Child of God?

http://www.HondurasChristianYouthMissions.org

www.ingramcontent.com/pod-product-compliance
Lightning Source LLC
Chambersburg PA
CBHW052018070526
44584CB00016B/1803